MW00876334

How To Start An Online Store

The Complete Step-by-Step Beginners Guide to Starting Your Online Business

Jonathan Eldridge and Robert Bustamante

Disclaimer

The following information is provided for information purposes only. Our opinion is given based on our experience and not to be considered legal or professional advice. Please consult with a qualified attorney, tax accountant, and other professionals to ensure you are proceeding correctly. Our information is provided as an opinion of our experience and we do not warrant, represent, or provide any guarantees as to the suitability or outcome you may have.

We reference and link to third party services. Some of these third party links are affiliate programs that we may be compensated for in the event you sign up. The use of these third party services does not guarantee any success and or earnings for your business. Furthermore, we do not guarantee any information, instruction, or opinion of these products or services. Readers are advised to do their own due diligence when deciding on a suitable company or fit for their business needs.

Readers of this book agree that Certatim, LLC, all officers and owners are not responsible for the success or failure of your business decisions related to any information provided in this book.

No part of this publication shall be transmitted, sold, or reproduced in whole or in part in any form, without the prior written consent of the author. All trademarks and registered trademarks appearing in this guide are the property of their respective owners.

Thank You

We want to thank you for the purchase of our book. We are two guys who have built hundreds of projects for clients and ourselves over the years.

What once required a team of professionals, is becoming easier and easier to do on your own. We hope that from reading this book, we will help dispel the myth that it is too hard to do yourself.

We want to save you time and money so that you can start your own online store immediately.

As an added gift we want to provide you with a downloadable resources guide at no additional charge. You can get this free downloadable guide at http://longlivetheinternet.com/book-gift

Lastly we have links throughout the book to various third party companies. Some of these we are compensated on and others we are not. Regardless they are all services we have used and are happy with. We greatly appreciate you clicking through them and giving them a try.

Jon & Bob from Long Live The Internet
http://www.longlivetheinternet.com

Table of Contents

Chapter 3 - Marketing and Off Site SEO

Monitoring Your Traffic
Who Is Sending You What Traffic
AdWords
Emails
Blogging
Backlinks
Offline Waste
Get Social
Google Alerts
Just Google It

Chapter 4 - Converting and Maximizing Your Revenue

Email Lists
The Drips
Offers And Urgency
Partnering And Affiliates
Trade Shows
Customer Service
You Made It

[1]

Getting Started

What is Ecommerce

THE INTERNET IS BY far the most revolutionary invention since electricity and arguably has changed the world forever. Information flows instantaneously from rebel revolts in Syria to Kim Kardashians Baby birth it now happens in real time. We are all exposed to news and information instantly. According to the International Telecommunications Union roughly 78% of the population in developed countries use the internet in some fashion.

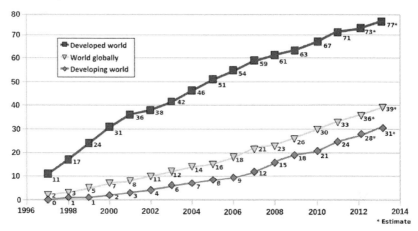

That makes just about 3 Billion people in the world using the internet. By 2017 60% of all U.S. retail sales will involve the internet in some way and approximately 10.3% of total retail sales in the U.S in five years will be online purchases. That's $370 billion in online sales.

Despite what you may think these online sales are being done by small businesses. Of course Amazon and the big boys are making up a large percentage but there is endless room for niche ecommerce sites catering to specific markets. There has never been a better time to start an ecommerce site and start building your future. Whether you start out full time or do this in the off hours after work, there is no reason that you can't build a successful online business if you stay committed.

We are going to outline the steps taken to do this. You don't need lots of money and you shouldn't be intimidated. We will walk you through the different steps and outline the tools and pitfalls that have helped us build half a dozen successful online businesses. Avoid the mistakes we made and you can launch in half the time and for half the cost.

Deciding What to Sell

When thinking about what you are going to sell there are a lot of considerations you need to think about. I was talking with a friend yesterday and he was very anxious and excited about launching an online store. We talked briefly about what he intended to offer and rather quickly it was apparent he had not thought through all the details. The first thing you need to consider is your interest in your idea. You love it now but can you love it for the long term. Regardless of the fact that you have an incredible deal, or a connection with an uncle who gets rabbit skins for deep discounts, doesn't necessarily mean you should be selling rabbit skins. In reality you are going to need to be committed to what you are intending to sell. Listing and starting your store is the beginning of a long road to great success. You are going to be intimately involved with your product or service. In order to effectively spread the word and market your store, you are going to need to socialize with people from this industry. You are going to need to partake in the communities whether online or at conferences, meetings or chat rooms related to your product or service. Do you really want to commit to rabbit skins. Is this your calling? If you answered yes, then at least you know you've thought it through.

After you decide on the topic or category that you are interested in, you need to think about logistics. If you plan on selling physical products like bikes or shirts or candy then you need to think about size and weight. Depending on your business plan or strategy there are a couple of options here from a logistics standpoint. Most people follow the conventional model of purchasing items, warehousing or storing them in their house and then selling them and shipping them once sold. As your company grows you may need more space to store these items. This is something to think about. If you are selling bikes online you are going to need a lot of space. You may even need to lease warehouse space. In addition to space you are going to need spend a lot of money on shipping and returns. According to a recent poll by 3Digital 93% of online shoppers say free shipping is the biggest source of encouragement to buy online. Can you afford to ship your bikes for free? Probably not.

Another option that you may consider is drop shipping. Drop shipping involves selling products online and letting a third party or the manufacturer directly ship the products to your client. This is a convenient and often cost saving option. There are some tradeoffs. Dropshipping can result in thinner margins of profit. Revenue splits with companies performing dropshipping for you can be expensive. In addition to slimmer profits, you are not in control of the product or packaging that is being sent. Packing, branding and mailing is a prime opportunity for you to build brand awareness, personalize the experience, and gain additional business by keeping your customer loyal.

A third option and one of the most exciting options is selling virtual products. A virtual product is either an ebook or online training course or access to a secure area of a website where additional information is available. This is one of the fastest growing areas of online sales and has exponential margins. Let's take this book as an example. While there are countless hours or writing and editing and years of online experience to draft this book, there are no recurring expenses. This means that once the book is written it can be sold in perpetuity for no large additional costs like a physical product may have.

Regardless of what you decide to sell, you want to make sure that you have thought through how you are going to do it. Do you enjoy the category you are targeting? How are you going to source or generate your product or service? Is it scalable and is there a large enough audience? Can you reach this audience? How are you going to handle the logistics? Do you have enough space in your house? Do you have more than one supplier in case your current one goes out of business? Take the time to think this through and don't be blinded by the opportunity. Launching your ecommerce site is going to take time and effort. Thinking through some of these things up front can save lots of headache down the road.

Defining Your Market

Part of effectively planning for success is thinking about your target market. Over the years we have built and released a number of online products without doing the required due diligence or research. We convinced ourselves we had; only to find that our targeted demographic was impossible to reach. When I say demographic I'm referring to your clients or customers. Who do you believe is your customer? What's their age? What's their taste? Where can you find them? Where do they frequent on and offline? Do you understand their desires or pain points? Can you relate to these people? Can they relate to you? You need to think through this in detail. Let's look at an example to dig further.

Let's say you wanted to start an online store selling horseback riding equipment. Most likely it is safe to assume that your demographic is going to be people that ride horses. They may or may not own a horse. Regardless they are probably active in the horse community both on and offline. For those that have been around horses for most of their life, clearly they are well equipped to offer products to this group of people. They have an intimate knowledge of what similar people think, where they go, forums they frequent and more.

However what if you aren't a horseback rider? What if you have no experience with the field? You need to think like a horse enthusiast and speak to them. You need to search online and see where these people congregate. Are there certification companies or organizations that you could use as a distribution channel? When browsing those sites who are your potential competitors? Do you see their advertisements on the site? What are they doing that looks appealing? What messages are they saying and who do they appear to be speaking to? Find your potential competitors and see what they are doing and saying. They are speaking to your demographic and probably doing a pretty good job. Concentrate on the leaders in the space and not the little guys. Lessons are learned from those that have done the work ahead of you.

The beauty of the internet is that it is endless and you don't need everyone to be your customer. There are a million fish in the sea and if you can carve a tiny niche of clients that aren't being targeted correctly or are looking for something new then you will have plenty of business.

Its important to think about your customer in depth. Let's look at another example. Let's say you were going to sell an ebook online titled "How To Learn To Horseback Ride In 10 Days." At first glance you may think that this is the same demographic as our last example. Arguably there may be some crossover but its actually a completely different demographic. In our first example we are targeting people who are active horseback riders. They are members of organizations and groups and they already ride. In this example we are targeting people looking to learn horseback riding.

These are beginners or people looking to get into horseback riding. The book may be better targeted to browsers of sites related to after school activities or hobbies or how to sites. If you rush to generalize you would assume they are the same demographic. Think a little further and you realize there's a slight difference that's extremely important. If you are chasing people to purchase your ebook on a site filled with experienced horseback riders, you are wasting your time and your money. Dig in and put yourself in your customers shoes.

Lastly you want to make sure that you are selecting a group or customer that is reachable. By reachable I am referring to being able to market to them and convey your sales pitch. If your target audience is anyone who breaths you are in trouble. That is too large of a potential customer and it is going to be too expensive to reach them. If you don't have a niche or a specific market you run the risk of being lost among the masses.

When Amazon launched they were an online bookstore. They only sold books and were able to make a niche for themselves. Now that they have reached critical mass they can offer everything. You can't try to appeal to everyone. Pick a niche and stick to it. Trying to please everyone will make your advertising and marketing more expensive and more difficult to focus. There is less competition and an easier chance of targeting horseback riders then there is of targeting everyone who likes outdoor sports.

What Do I Need to Start

What do you really need to start your online business? This is a tricky question because everyone has different goals for how they want to start. Some people want to raise millions of dollars to have a huge launch party and open with a bang. This book is not for them. This book is focused on starting small and organically growing your business to a large one. Often people refer to the adages that first impressions are everything or you only get one chance to make a first impression. While this is true, there are close to 3 Billion internet users in the world. This really means you have 3 Billion chances to make a first impression. It is better to have something online with some chance of making something than it is to have nothing up and no chance of selling anything. What I'm saying is start small. Who cares? Open an online store with one product if that is all you can afford to start with. Is someone not going to buy from you because you only offer that product? Maybe some won't but maybe some will. If they want that one product and you've made a convincing argument they will buy it. You have to start somewhere.

Just 10 years ago, launching an online business may have cost upwards of $10,000 to get started. I am telling you that you can start an online business with $500 and a lot of your time. I'm not going to tell you that you just need $500 and you are done. You have to be committed to the project and to making it happen. You directly receive what you put into it. If you aren't prepared to invest your time then this is not going to work. Save your $500. Now $500 is not going to work or be appropriate for most of you. You may have access to more capital and want to start a little bigger to be able to have more products or advertise in more areas but I'm saying it is not required. We have started multiple projects with anywhere from $500 to $3000 in allocated funds for it and have grown them into million dollar businesses.

A fair budget really depends on your product, and your arrangement with your suppliers. Maybe you are starting an online shoe company and the shoe store down the street is willing to make a deal with you. You list the shoes online and when they sell, you buy them from them at a little more than the wholesale rate and send it to your customer. This saves you the expense of inventorying all the shoes and sizes and frees up that capital. The shoe store is also pleased as they are selling more shoes and moving inventory for a smaller profit but a profit nonetheless. You may also be writing an ebook. If you are planning on selling your ebook then you have no cost to your inventory. Your cost was the time that you already invested to write the book or spent to have someone else write the book. From our experience if you are looking at a smaller size store with some basic inventory for a reasonably priced product you can probably be comfortable with $2k to $3k. This is not required but probably a good start.

So now you have your money, but what else are you going to need? You are going to need a computer with internet access. I highly recommend that you have high speed internet access and a trusty computer. These two items are possibly the most important parts of your business. You will be running, communicating, and building your business from your computer. In addition to your computer a portable smartphone will give you the flexibility of working or responding to email from anywhere. This is not required, but can be helpful for a ton of tasks you will need to perform. You can handle your banking, accept credit cards, receive support calls, and respond to emails from anywhere. Lastly a printer that doesn't gobble ink. With a computer, internet connection, a printer, a phone and a bank account with at least $500 you are now ready to get started. In the next chapter we start getting to work so take a break, relax and get ready to roll up your sleeves.

Setting Goals and Priorities

Getting started can feel like a daunting task and speaking to friends and family can often make it worse. Human nature is that people want you to do well; but, not better than them. With that said you will hear many people tell you why your idea is going to fail. Now I'm not going to say to ignore all those things. There is often a lot of truth in the feedback that you receive. Most of the time they may actually be correct but, you need to take it all with a grain of salt. Is the person qualified to be giving their opinion? Are they in business for themselves already? I have a tremendous amount of respect and highly weigh the credibility of people who are already successfully in business for themselves. If you haven't started something or run something yourself then you really don't know what it takes. It doesn't mean your feedback isn't relevant or valuable. It just means that further consideration should be given to feedback from those that have done it rather than those who haven't.

Talk through your idea and speak to pessimists. You want to be as knowledgeable as possible about pitfalls and make sure that you have a viable answer for all scenarios or problems people throw at you. Hard work can solve a lot of problems but don't ignore the glaring issues with your idea. When you answer the critique think again about what you said. Does it make sense? Bounce your idea off people. Opinions are often wrong but there is usually something to learn from it. Sometimes it can help you see your mission with more clarity.

Lastly when explaining the idea try taking yourself out of the equation. Say that you have a friend that is thinking about doing x or y and what do you think about that. You will get a more honest opinion of the idea than if you said you are doing it yourself. People sometimes tell you what you want to hear and not what they truly think. If you take yourself out of the equation you often get better advice.

So you've decided on an idea and decided on the product or service you are going to sell. Now it is time to define your goals. This is where most people go awry. You may disagree with me here and many people do. I feel adamantly that if you are organized and think things through, than creating a business plan is a waste of time. Unless you plan on raising money and presenting your idea to people, it is a complete waste of time. I understand that a business plan helps you foresee problems and get organized. Theoretically it helps you think about your market and strategy for success. All of these things are true but don't necessarily require you to write a formal elaborate business plan.

You're already reading this book and if you're reading this book, chances are that you've read plenty of other online forums and opinions about starting an ecommerce site. A business plan lets you justify delaying what you ultimately want to do which is launch or start your business now. If you aren't raising money then stop your business plan now. It makes for a good school project but not something that gets you to market quickly. Create a goal and outline the steps to get there. Arbitrary revenue projections mean nothing and you shouldn't waste your time with them.

The overall goal or launching your ecommerce business is just that. Launching your ecommerce business. Now there are a couple of theories about when to launch but I tend to fall somewhere in the middle of the two. Let me explain further. Similar to children there are two schools of thought. Some children if given a bowl of candy will eat the entire bowl immediately and others will save the candy to be eaten later or in multiple sittings. These personalities are different but there isn't one that's necessarily right or wrong. You could argue both sides.

When planning your ecommerce site you are going to need to decide when is right for you. Do you launch your site quickly without all your inventory and without all the features and Knick knacks you want or do you continue to tinker on the site and adjust the hue of the pink over and over only to never launch? Like I said, I feel that you probably want to fall somewhere in between. You need to understand that there is never a perfect time and there is never a perfect site. It is more important to get your site up and iterate from there. You see once you launch you can continue to work on the site.

So you say, "I got it. I need to launch and not drag my feet but what does that mean." That means that with a broad stroke I'm going to say that it shouldn't take more than three months to launch something. This is going to be a crazy hectic time but with kids, and homework and possibly a full time job and other responsibilities you can still do this. As long as you stay committed you can make it happen. Now I understand some of you are saying I'm crazy and you don't understand how much I have to do and other responsibilities I have and other commitments. You're right. I don't know your specific case and all the responsibilities you have but these are excuses. You have heard this before.

> *"If you need something done, give it to someone busy and they will make it happen."*

We aren't looking for excuses, we're looking for action and solutions. If you tell yourself you are never going to do it then you won't. You can make it happen but we can't make it happen for you.

One of the most important steps to making it happen for me is organizing with a To-Do list. It sounds so basic and simple but if you don't have a list of priorities and items to address then you are working frantically in a million directions without a plan. There are a lot of different online tools that you can use to keep your lists and stay organized. Trello is an option that people love that allows you to group and organize your to dos and ideas. It is free and worth looking at. Other people use a simple todo list offered in Gmail or Microsoft Outlook. These will work also but honestly my to-do list of choice is an old school notepad.

I know it sounds silly as I outline your successful path to launching an ecommerce site but there is something to be said about a tactile piece of paper or notepad. This allows me to be able to glance down from the computer and look at. Additionally there is a small sense of accomplishment that I personally get from physically checking something off the list. A good trusty old school notepad goes a long way. Regardless of what you decide on, staying organized with a list is crucial. This way you don't lose track of the ultimate goal.

> *"The big picture is launching and all the other items are little to-dos along the way."*

The first step is to start with a list of all the imaginable things you are going to have to do. This should be a comprehensive list from deciding on a name and designing your logo to sourcing your products and images. To give you some ideas we have included this list as a starting point. Each business is a little different and therefore will have a completely different list but this should give you an idea of the types of things to put on your list.

- [ ] Define your startup capital $$
- [ ] Decide on a name
- [ ] Register your domain name
- [ ] Setup your email
- [ ] File your corporate paperwork
- [ ] Get a federal Tax id EIN
- [ ] Register with the State for Sales Tax
- [ ] Setup your bank account
- [ ] Fund your account
- [ ] Get checks and debit/credit card
- [ ] Get a phone number
- [ ] Decide on an accounting strategy
- [ ] Design your logo
- [ ] Define your color palette and site style
- [ ] Decide on your sales platform
- [ ] Setup your online sales platform
- [ ] Get a launch static page up with email opt-in
- [ ] Start letting people know you are working on your project
- [ ] Decide on payment processing and apply
- [ ] Compile a list of Brands/Suppliers
- [ ] Contact the brands to determine requirements and ordering terms
- [ ] Compile a breakdown of initial intended products and cost allocation
- [ ] Make sure your list has enough assortment and variations (sizes,types)
- [ ] Determine if vendor has product photos or you are responsible
- [ ] Place vendor orders
- [ ] Start compiling product photos

- ☐ Resize photos and remove backgrounds or standardize
- ☐ Get additional images or logos from vendors
- ☐ Register all your social network accounts
- ☐ Start writing original product descriptions
- ☐ Start adding products to your platform
- ☐ Decide on packaging and shipping and order materials
- ☐ Order business cards or flyers
- ☐ Create a Google analytics account
- ☐ Start creating backlinks while researching
- ☐ Write a blog post or two about getting started and yourself
- ☐ Define a launch date and start building hype socially
- ☐ Compile a list of friends and family emails
- ☐ Create a friends and family discount code
- ☐ Open your site
- ☐ Send an email announcement to everyone you know
- ☐ Update status on all social network sites
- ☐ Submit your site to Google for indexing
- ☐ Make a schedule for social updates
- ☐ Ask friends for referrals
- ☐ Setup Google AdWords account and other CPC campaigns
- ☐ Create backlinks socially and other ways
- ☐ Monitor your funds and reconcile books
- ☐ Create list of local sales opportunities or events
- ☐ Create a list of partnership organizations
- ☐ Rinse and repeat all of your content, product updates, blogging and social sharing

[2]
Building Your Ecommerce Business

YOU'VE GATHERED THE courage and the appropriate capital and resources and you're out of excuses. It is time to dive in and get started. So let's do this.

Deciding on a Name

Let's start with something fun. Let's start with a name for your new venture. This is the part that most people enjoy. While this is an enjoyable job, you shouldn't take longer than a couple of days to decide on a name and move forward. You can't get caught on this stage because frankly it is not the most important thing. This can however suck the life from you. Below is a story that shows a little of my thought process in naming your company. This story is about an online service we no longer own but touches on a lot of important factors to consider and gives you some ideas.

"When we started crow tracker and the concept of tracking employee's location, we realized that essentially we had millions of options for names. Most of the possible ideas sounded boring or generic. Track My Employee, Employee GPS Tracker, Where are My Employees, Dude Where's My Car, Where oh Where, As the Crow Flies, Employee Location Tracker, Employee Tracker, and the list goes on and on with other candidates.

We wanted something different. Something memorable and maybe with a hint of clever. In addition we historically named our products or companies with animals or colors so as to create something easy to remember. You don't want someone telling their friend they use "Track My Employee" only to never remember that generic meaningless name again. Was it Track My Employee or Employee Tracker or GPS Tracking blah blah blah. I feel that if the name has something like a color or animal in it, it makes it easier to spell, remember and hopefully refer.

Ok so now we needed a color or animal and something memorable or clever. Quite a few of us in the office were watching Game of Thrones at the time. In Game of Thrones, they use an elaborate system of crow couriers. These crows deliver messages from one location or castle across the land to another. The idea is they were quick and could travel directly without terrain concerns from one point to another.

This concept is where the expression "As the Crow Flies" comes from. Wikipedia states that As the crow flies is an idiom for the shortest path or route between any two points. The saying "As the Crow Flies" has been around, or apparently appears in print, as early as 1758. Eureka, we had found an animal and concept that related nicely to the concept of locating your employees or tracking your people. It was short, succinct, a little clever (not all that much) and was an easy to spell memorable animal. But one last problem existed. It's the problem that all new business go through when deciding on a name.

We need a domain name. Now it sounds crazy to think that an obscure combination of loosely somewhat unaffiliated names could possibly already be registered. You would be surprised to see how often it does. Monkey Dancer. Yeah someone owns it. Purple Dinosaur. Yup. As the crow flies dot com. That one also. Lastly it must be a .com. We are not interested in .us or other useless domain extensions. Trackmyemployeegps.org. Not so much. So off we went to see if the name had been taken. Voila it was available. We plunked down our ten bucks and it was ours. www.crowtracker.com"

While this story is about an online service and not relevant to your ecommerce site, its shows you some of the things we think are integral in naming your company. Is it easy to remember, easy to differentiate from the crowd, easy to spell and most importantly the domain name available?

Registering Your Domain Name

Please don't decide on your name and create your company before you have the domain name. I don't care how clever or perfect your company name is. If you can't get a good domain name then it won't matter. You are building an ecommerce business and the domain name is the most important way people find you. As you saw in the last story, there are a number of things to consider. You don't want to be cute with the spelling of your domain name. Think about telling someone the domain name of your site and then think what your next sentence is. If the next sentence out of your mouth is how to spell it you're making a mistake with your domain name. You don't want to have to explain to everyone how to spell your site. You don't want a dash in your name. You don't want a .net or .us or anything that people are going to forget. Stick with a .com.

There are a couple of things to consider when choosing your domain name related to search engine optimization. We will get into this in more detail later but search engine optimization is how you are able to control factors that result in where your site shows up in search engines. When people search for Motorcycle Helmets and you are an online store offering motorcycle helmets you want to appear higher in the search results. There is a direct correlation between traffic and how high you rank in the results. I don't want to lose you here but the reason I bring it up is because we believe that your domain name is one of the factors considered in the ranking of your site for various terms. This is a debatable argument and you will find just as many people online saying it does matter as those saying it doesn't. I'm telling you from testing on dozens of sites, it helps. It's not a game changer but it helps. This means that www.motorcyclehelmets.com generally speaking would have a better chance of showing higher in the search results than www.chipsheadprotection.com when searching for "motorcycle helmets."

Now you need to actually search for the domain name availability and register it. Head over to GoDaddy. Its simple and inexpensive. You just need a domain name and if you also would like another layer of privacy you can add privacy to the domain registration for an additional $15 or $20. We would recommend doing this otherwise your address and name will be visible from a domain whois lookup. Its not a huge issue but you may not want to show your home address online. Make sure when you are registering your domain not to add anything like hosting or email or other unnecessary items. We will discuss these items later but at this time you do not need to upgrade anything unless you want to add the optional privacy protection.

When registering your domain name you going to be asked to select the number of years you would like to register the domain for. There are a number of search engine professionals who are now saying that this is another factor that Google is using to rank your site. They believe that a longer registration or more time remaining on the registration period implies permanence and therefore is a more reliable site.

Reliable site = Rank higher on search results

We can't say this is true for sure but it is something to consider when registering your domain name. A happy medium between cost and this concern may be to register your domain for 2 or 3 years. It is not a large expense more and gives you peace of mind that you don't need to worry about it for some time.

Setting Up Your Email

You have your domain name so now let's set up your email. This is a really important step that so many new business don't do. It is important to look and act big even if you are a one man operation. The beauty of the internet is that nobody actually knows how big or small you are unless of course you show them. Having a personalized email is the easiest way to pass the sniff test. There is nothing worse than getting a business card and seeing the persons email address as suziesmall@hotmail.com. It just shows that you are a small operation and looks unprofessional. Now there are a lot of ways to accomplish this and you may want to get the email from GoDaddy directly but my personal recommendation after having used many different options is to signup for Google Apps for Business.

Google Apps for business is built on their Gmail platform. Gmail is the most widely used web based email provider with over 425 million active users worldwide. Google Apps will allow you to easily use your domain name to create email aliases or groups. For example if your name is Suzy Queen you can create any email address you want like suzyq@yourdomainname.com or suzy@yourdomainname.com. You will also be able to setup a support alias or a shop alias or anything you want like returns@yourdomainname.com. You can also set these up and just have them forward to one email address. This way you can give the appearance that you have multiple departments when they are all routing to you. Google apps also comes with a whole suite of other features like a calendar and the ability to connect to Microsoft Outlook if you prefer to use Outlook to send and receive emails.

> WARNING <

Google apps email comes with a default mail setting that confuses most users. Its called conversation view and it groups messages with the same subject together in clusters. It makes for a confusing cluster of emails that don't appear in one chronological list in your inbox online. This feature can be disabled. Click on settings and turn conversation view off. Some people prefer the grouped emails but its different than what most users are accustomed to.

All that aside, we couldn't function without google apps. We run various different businesses with different domain names and over a hundred aliases with Google Apps. The cost is $5 per user account per month and is worth all 17 cents a day you pay for it. Proficient users once comfortable will save considerable time responding to emails with keyboard shortcuts. Additionally everything can be done from web based access to your email from anywhere with an internet connection. They have great apps for android and iPhone as well as easily integrating to all the other Google services we will be discussing later in the book. Look around and consider other options, but to me there is no choice.

Forming a Company

The legal creation of your company is often considered a difficult step and one that people spend too much time and too much money on. I'm giving you the disclaimer that we're not attorneys or tax professionals and should you feel the need to consult with them, you absolutely should. With the disclaimer aside, you may find that speaking with an experienced family member or friend may do as well. They may actually be able to give you similar advice without paying unnecessary fees. We have always structured our new endeavors as LLCs or Limited Liability Companies. The benefit of this structure is that its treated as a corporate entity and responsible for filing a tax return at the end of the year but the income or expenses flow through to your personal tax return. The LLC acts an independent entity that is responsible for its actions and has limited exposure up to the amount of assets the company has. This gives you the benefits of a company without the complexity of a corporation. Like I said you may want to consult with a professional to determine this decision for yourself. If you don't have someone to speak to, search the internet as there are countless resources to explain the differences to you.

Once you have decided on the corporate entity you are going to create, please think twice before paying an attorney $500 or more to file the paperwork. I live in Florida and am not sure of the process in all states but most states have a division of corporations. This is the State agency responsible for granting licenses and forming a company. In the state of Florida you would go to the Division of Corporations website to file your paperwork. You can look on the site to find the link to create a new company regardless of your structure. Their online process lets you complete the entire process in about 15 minutes and $150 in State filing fees. Once you complete this online process you are officially in business. There is no waiting time or holding period. You can file and be open in 15 minutes.

So now you are ready for business right? Not so fast there. Don't forget about your taxes. Your next step is to register with federal government to get your Tax ID number. Your Tax ID is used to file and pay federal taxes. You need to call and get your EIN or Employment Identification Number also referred to as a Tax ID. This number is the equivalent of a Social Security number for companies. You will use this number at the end of the year to file your taxes. Its your company federal identification number. Getting an EIN number is simple and fast. You can do it online or over the phone and the agency is actually open late on most nights. You will want to search for EIN online and make sure you are going to an IRS website. Don't fall for sites that look similar. It should be the actual IRS website.

Once you have completed your EIN registration you will need to go to your State tax authority and register to pay State sales taxes. It is important to familiarize yourself with your specific States tax policies. For example selling digital products in Florida has different tax implications from physical products. Additionally the location of your customer and where the sale is made affects the rate. Each State has their own tax laws and you should research this directly on the States website. If you are unsure pick up the phone and call them or send them an email. You would be surprised how helpful they are. In Florida the entity is the Florida Department of Revenue. Registering with the state should be your last step as most state authorities will require your Division of Corporations company number as well as your EIN to setup your account. "What the #$%@!," you are saying. Relax. Take a breath. This process is not as difficult as it sounds and there are extensive details on many of these websites to help people you through the process if you get stuck.

> **WARNING <**
There are many companies charging fees on top of state and federal agencies for services and add ons that you don't need. Make sure that the website you go to is actually a State or Federal website. Furthermore, you will receive mail after creating your company with official looking documents and stationery. Read the small print as most of them are not State or Federal agencies but rather third parties offering unnecessary services. Throw them out.

Setting Up Your Bank Account

This not our specialty but having a number of businesses and accounts at a number of different banking establishments I thought I would provide my experience with this particular decision. Banking seems to be one of those personal topics and decisions that people don't openly discuss. It's strange that people are secretive about it but a weird observation nonetheless. The old school mentality of banking, involved dressing up in nice clothes to go meet with the neighborhood bank manager. Here you would sit with a representative and interview to setup an account or apply for a loan. I'm not implying that this relationship doesn't to this day in parts of the country, but banking overall has become far less personal. As banks look to maximize profits, they do this by reducing expenses. If they can keep you from speaking with tellers or employees, they need less employees. Less employees cuts their expenses and benefits their bottom line. As a result banks are putting more and more services online or in apps.

I understand that neighborhood and local banks offer a level of support that you may not get from a larger bank. The truth is, I don't need it. If you live in an area of the country where Bank of America is available, I would highly recommend them. You are able to create an account, apply for a loan, deposit checks, transfer funds, and just about any other banking transaction from the comfort of your home. A small neighborhood bank can't offer technology and features that a large bank can. I understand this may not work for everyone and everyone has different things that are important for them. All that aside, the convenience of handling various different requests quickly and without much fanfare works for us.

Accounting

You're yawning already aren't you? Stop. This is important and often overlooked. You may not need to know the intricacies of the tax code and detailed exemptions. However, you must have a grasp of your company's finances. You are planning on launching a lean company and every dollar is going to matter. You need to know how much you have at any time. Nobody other than yourself should be responsible for this. Forget the fact that you may not be good at math or interested in it. Those are excuses and if you can't handle your money, then you shouldn't be launching a company. Get it together and learn. It is not so tough. The money you make is income and the money you spend are expenses. Income minus expenses equals profits.

So how are you going to track these expenses and make sure you don't overspend or overdraft your account? I would highly recommend QuickBooks. We have been using QuickBooks for years now but in the last couple of years they have rolled out a new online version. This online version allows you to connect to your Bank Account and actually suck in all the transactions from your bank automatically. This saves countless time of data input. Once a week you can login and classify the income and expenses that have already been automatically added for your review into your QuickBooks account.

Regardless of how you do it, you need to stay current and get this in order from the get go. Delaying and waiting is only going to snowball the problem. Starting is easy and once you have an organized system, you can rest well at night knowing it is current, accurate, and managed.

Getting a Phone Number

The days of landlines are quickly coming to an end. While there are still some benefits to having a landline, they are far exceeded by the portability of new virtual numbers and features that exist with them. When we discuss virtual numbers we are talking about computer controlled numbers that you can route to any phone or voicemail you would like. There are a number of services available and we have used many of them. For the purpose of an ecommerce site our recommendation to you is to register for a Google voice phone number.

Google offers a free service that not many people know about. Go to Google Voice and signup for your account. Here you will be able to select a phone number from a list of numbers that they own. Once setup you can forward this number to your personal phone whether your cell or a landline. This way the number is virtual. You don't have to give your personal phone number out and you are able to see all calls coming from this phone number. This lets you answer with your corporate message as opposed to your personal calls when someone is calling from this personalized number. Google Voice comes with a host of other features including voicemail that you can setup just for the company as well as transcribed messages that are emailed to your inbox if you miss the call. The features are incredible and for free you can't beat it.

If you have a number of different people that are going to be involved with your initial launch and you feel you need something a little more robust out of the gate, we still recommend you go with a virtual number. Two different providers we have used are OneBox and Ring Central. Both of these are very powerful allowing you to create custom phone trees and directing various extensions to other peoples phones. This allows you to look like a large operation but are actually just forwarding calls to other cell phones or land lines. You will want to check each providers available numbers for your desired area code though before you sign up as they both have limited inventories of various area codes.

Creating your Logo

Getting a logo is one of those things that can often take way too much time. It is fun like coming up with your name and that is why most people spend so much time with it. There are a number of different routes you take to get your logo designed. You can hire a professional marketing company and talk about the feel and audience and then waste time and money on consumer polls and other nonsense. Alternatively you can decide what you like and decide what you don't and compile that into a description of your ideal logo. From here you will take this description to have it created.

If you are more of a DIY type you should head over to Pixellogo. Here you can browse through 1000's of options and sort them accordingly. For a reasonable price $30 to $40 you can purchase a logo file and then modify the words and colors if you so choose to match your look and desired feel.

If you are looking for something more customized I would recommend you take a look at 99 Designs. 99 Designs allows you to host your own contest. It is more expensive and starts at about $250. You will define what you are looking for in a logo and your likes and dislikes and then people will submit their designs for your review. You can thumbs up and thumbs down until you narrow it down to a finalized logo of your choosing.

The last option and most affordable is to go to Fiverr. This site lets you shop through thousands of different services from people online mostly from developing countries for $5. You would then look at their work and provide your description to guide them in creating your logo. It may take 2 or 3 sellers to find one that really creates what you are looking for.

> **WARNING** <

This site does have a lot of poor quality vendors but there are tons of amazing vendors. You have to dig through and review the work. I can't tell you the number of things we have done through Fiverr. We had a personalized video from Professor Von Puppet made and a launch photo for our online jewelry store shown below as well as the formatting of this book and countless other marketing and SEO services. Check peoples reviews and don't be the first person to try someone out. Go with people who have been reviewed positively before.

Professor Von Puppet

Launch Image

What Type of Site Should It Be

You have a name, a logo, a corporate entity and now it is time to truly define the type of site you are going to launch. It is important to think about all of the different types of websites that exist online and consider them as options. Ecommerce no longer specifically refers to a traditional website where you sell a bunch of products that you can add to your shopping cart. In fact there are now many different types of sites online, all essentially utilizing e commerce. There are basically four types of sites that we are going to touch on here. These four types of sites can be broken down as follows: Blogs, Landing Pages, Forums, and Shopping Sites.

Blogs

Defined as an informational or discussion forum where one or a few people publish content online. Updates can be made daily, weekly, or as often as the writer wants. Blogging has become extremely popular over the years and has allowed people to easily post their thoughts, news or other information to a regular set of readers. After building a following, many bloggers have looked to monetize their sites. This can be done from a number of ways including banner advertisements, referral programs, or even selling their own related products alongside their blog.

There are a number of different platforms that you can use to easily setup a blog including Blogger and the most popular WordPress. WordPress is the largest blogging platform and is free. There are millions of WordPress sites and given its success over the years it makes it our recommended platform of choice. WordPress can be hosted for free at wordpress.com with advertising. If you are going to launch a professional looking site we would recommend hosting it yourself though with a hosting company. One of the largest and easiest to setup is Blue Host which offers WordPress setup and hosting for less than $10 a month.

WordPress is an extremely powerful platform designed for beginner to intermediate users with simple updates available from a pretty easy to use admin section. You don't need to be a programmer to get around with this. There are thousands and thousands of powerful free extensions that can be installed by beginners and this makes for a great option for those looking to blog. WordPress does not come out of the box with ecommerce functionality and you would need to look at the ecommerce plugins available (there are hundreds) to add payments to your WordPress site. This option is best if you want to first start a blog and build up an audience with the intention of adding ecommerce down the road. WordPress is a no-brainer. You can go to Blue Host and signup and they will set the whole thing up for you in minutes including WordPress.

Landing Pages

A landing page is one or a couple of rich pages solely created to drive the guest to opt into an email or to purchase a product. These are generally highly focused pages with the sole intent of defining the product or service, showing endorsements, addressing any concerns and converting the guest to the desired outcome. You will often see free giveaways for opting into an email list and then the sale is made over time through and email drip campaign. We will discuss email drips later in the book.

Landing pages have evolved substantially over the years. With the popularity of social media, it's become extremely important to show social endorsements though for your product or service. People want to see what others are saying about your product on various different platforms. We have been using a site called LeadPages and are very happy with the results. This site is designed for beginners and allows you to easily drag and drop elements to customize your specific landing page.

You can chose from pre made landing page templates. The best feature is that they show you the conversion rates of all the different templates of landing pages. They share the data from all of their other users and you are able to see what percentage of people opt in or purchase from each different template type. Lead Pages offers a ton of different templates for email opt in pages, video training platforms and other options that focus on the sale of a single product or class or service. They have been thoroughly tested by thousands of users and most are optimized to look good on smart phones as well as desktop computers. If you are thinking about selling an ebook or a training class, this is a great option for you.

Forums

Users come to share their thoughts with one another about various different topics of discussion. This type of site can take time to build an audience and group of people who support the community. There are many successful forums with specific topics they cover creating a highly focused group of engaged users. Forum owners try and monetize their site similar to a blog with advertising, referral programs, or direct E Commerce of a specific product or service tailored to their audience.

A forum is a little more involved in setting up or maintaining but the easiest way to do this and one that we would recommend is to setup a WordPress hosting site at BlueHost and actually install the plugin called BuddyPress. BuddyPress is a Wordpress add-on that converts your Wordpress site into a forum where people can register and comment as well as thousands of other features. BuddyPress is free. There are thousands of successful online forums powered by BuddyPress and this will allow you to setup a forum with limited to no technical experience.

Shopping Sites

The last of the four options we will look at is a conventional shopping site. This is a product driven store with a shopping cart and the standardized model of purchasing items online. This particular type is the one we will spend most time focusing on throughout the book. This is the traditional store model.

There are now a whole host of options to build your online store but we are going to focus on our favorite here which is Shopify. In addition to Shopify there are other options like Volusion, Yahoo Stores and simple options like an eBay or Etsy store. While these other options can be both limiting and powerful we feel that Shopify offers the perfect balance of beginner and customization options allowing you to look professional with very little experience.

Shopify powers over a 100k online ecommerce stores and allows you to setup, configure, and launch an ecommerce site, accepting payments in a week. Setting up an account can take 10 minutes and you will have a default template or layout for your site immediately. While the default layout is beautiful and can suffice, I recommend spending a little bit more money to purchase a responsive template so that your users get a great experience regardless of the device they are using whether a desktop, tablet, or phone.

Site Design

We're not going to spend a considerable amount of time on design because this can be subjective. What we like, you may hate, and what you hate, we may love. We are going to focus on elements that we think are crucial regardless of whether you believe your page should be purple or black. While you are working on your site you will need to at least have a splash page up to welcome users.

Coming Soon Launch Page

The first thing you are going to want to do is put up a "coming soon" page. I'm not referring to the pages you remember seeing with flashing barricades. You at least want something that helps build the hype and more importantly starts building your email list. Later on in the marketing section we will talk in more detail about selecting an email marketing company and some of the options available. For now lets assume you have already decided on your email delivery provider. This is not to be confused with your internal company email provider but actually the company you are going to use to send newsletters or upsell messages or specials.

Your main objective for your launch page is to tease the visitor with a little information and to collect email addresses for the launch of your site. There are a number of options for you to easily put this together and the largest one out there is LaunchRock. They offer a free or paid version with different functionality. Launch Rock lets you easily setup a launch page collecting emails. You will want to make sure you are connecting your email collection to your email provider and launch rock will walk you through this for the major providers. If you are using a hosted shopping cart solution like Shopify they have a built in coming soon page that you can modify to your liking and customize the colors etc. You will want to add a link to sign up for your email list and connect that to a link you will obtain from your email provider.

The Actual Site

When designing your site you need to remember to focus on what is important. Your ultimate goal is to make your site simple and easy to use. I can't stress the importance of this. You would be surprised how many sites have trouble executing on this. You want to design with the intention of removing obstacles. When someone is ready to checkout or pay let them do so. Below is a list of some design principles we find important.

- The top of every page should have a link to your shopping cart.
- Buttons should be large and clear to read
- Input boxes should be large and easy to enter your information
- Less is more. Don't be wordy when you don't need to on payment pages
- Don't require a full account registration to make a payment.
- Repeat your navigation in the footer of the website
- Make sure your logo at the top of the page always links to the homepage
- Use large wording where you can
- If you have dark backgrounds use light text and vice versa

There are obviously hundreds of other things to consider from a cosmetic standpoint but this is a list of items we consistently see on other sites. You need to make sure you address these simple fixes.

Mobile design is something that has emerged over the last couple of years and something I think everyone needs to consider at this point. What I'm referring is the concept of making your website responsive.

What is Responsive?
Responsive web design customizes the display of your site for each type of device. For example an iPhone will receive one view and a desktop user on a large screen will receive a different view that is optimized for the larger screen. Responsive web design is not a mobile app that you have to download from the app store.

People are using smartphones more often than their desktop computers and if your site is not easily browsed on a phone, people will go elsewhere. While it is tough to give an exact number of smartphone users, it is clear that more and more users are using smartphones to shop and make purchases online. We are seeing sales of more than 50% being performed on a smart phone. That is a fact that can't be ignored and one you should consider up front. While this may sound complicated, don't be afraid. When building your site you can purchase responsive themes. I would recommend you highly consider a responsive theme. It is going to convert shoppers more easily and will save lots of time and headache in the future when you ultimately realize you need one.

Online Payments

You have to decide the type of site you are going to build and the platform that you are going to run it on. Separate from the platform you are going to accept payments and you will need to decide how you are going to do this. This part can seem scary and confusing but it shouldn't be.

There are two different parties involved in collecting payments online. There is the gateway provider and the merchant company. You need both of these in order to collect payments online. A payment gateway is the company that actually receives the credit card information from your site. They are the party responsible for verifying that there is money on the card and that the charge is acceptable. Once the charge goes through, the merchant company is actually the one who acts as a bank. The merchant company handles the transfer of the money from the credit card company to your bank account.

Conveniently in the last couple of years there are new providers that actually act as both the gateway company and the merchant company. You can use Stripe which is a streamlined payment system that acts as both your merchant and gateway provider and of course PayPal. PayPal is widely used and trusted and handles both payments for you. You may think that PayPal checkout often looks unprofessional and this may be true for some peoples integrations. PayPal actually offers various solutions which allow you to customize that experience for your users. You don't have to use the basic version. But don't be so quick to change it. A recent study performed by comScore showed that PayPal users were more than twice as likely to complete their purchases and check out than were shoppers who used other checkout and payment options.

Depending on the ecommerce solution you chose to handle your site, you will have different options. The rates do differ slightly from processor to processor and you should educate yourself here as you can save some pocket change. Our recommendations is Authorize.net.

> **> WARNING <**
> Don't drive yourself nuts shopping for the best deal in town. The pricing structures are so complicated that you are probably not going to be comparing apples to apples once you have your information. I recommend you go with the big boys that dominate the space as they are competitive and fair.

WordPress or Generic Shopping Cart Solution

If you are building a WordPress site or other platform and have picked a shopping cart solution then chances are it integrates with Authorize.net. Authorize.net is the largest processor of payments online and we have a partner link here for you to sign up. Click Here .We have used them on half a dozen of our sites. We have found them to be fair and honest. They are the gateway providers and they will assign you a merchant company for convenience. Generally the merchant companies they send are all comparable but if you have decided on your own merchant provider you would just let Authorize know. We use Merchant Focus and you can actually get a $50 credit if you sign up at this link and enter this promo code: **F91163D6**

If you go with Authorize.net or another gateway company they will setup Visa and MasterCard out of the gate. American Express is a different creature and you will need to contact American Express directly to apply for a merchant account. American Express will check your credit and once approved will provide you with a merchant number. You will provide this number to Authorize or your gateway company of choice so that you can take American Express as well.

In addition to Visa, MasterCard and American Express I believe that offering PayPal is a huge way to increase your potential purchasers. Some reports are showing as high as a 30% increase in sales when they added the ability to pay with PayPal. Its an additional option that many people look for because of convenience and security concerns. Recently Google has offered Google Checkout and Apple has launched Apple Pay. These two are a little new and its still too early to see the benefit of them in my opinion. You also want to avoid cluttering your checkout with options which often results in further indecision and abandoned carts.

Lastly if you have decided on Shopify for your ecommerce store we recommend you use their payment system. It uses Stripe but is handled directly through Shopify. I highly recommend this route as it saves you a lot of time and aggravation with setting up your own account and handles the American Express portion as well. Directly through Shopify you can sign up to take PayPal, Visa, MasterCard and American Express all in one streamlined process. If we haven't made it clear, we want to reiterate that Shopify is by far the easiest way to launch your site online if you are building a traditional e commerce site. We have used and launched dozens of sites all with different solutions from Magento to custom developed cart integrations and if you are starting your first endeavor there is no easier way to go.

Keeping an Eye On On-Site SEO

This could be boring but is probably one of the most important sections we are going to talk about for the future success of your online company. Times have changed and old school marketing efforts are expensive, often ineffective, and irrelevant to e commerce businesses.

What is SEO? SEO stands for Search Engine Optimization. SEO means optimizing your website both on-site and off-site to make sure that search engines can find you. Hopefully, in return, these search engines will present your site to people when searching for what you are selling. Unfortunately SEO is often clouded in secrecy and viewed with skepticism and doubt. I'm here to tell you it works and it is not as magical as many would like you to believe. The bottom line is that optimization improves your rankings and results in your site showing higher on the list of search results.

There is a direct correlation to the amount of traffic that you receive and your rank for different search terms. Googles success as a search engine is based around their algorithm that is tightly guarded and secretive. Google has fine-tuned their formula for determining the most relevant sites for each search. While Google will not disclose exactly how they rank sites, they have provided lots of information and guidance. Applying this guidance works and will help your site show above others when searching online.

What is a Keyword? A keyword is a word or string of words that you believe is relevant to your site. For example if you sell bow ties for men, a good keyword would be "mens bow ties" or "bow ties for men."

Keywords
We mentioned keywords briefly when talking about naming your company. Hopefully your name or domain name has some semblance of your ideal keyword but it doesn't have to. Your bow tie company may be named Joes Things and your domain name www.joesthings.com but it would help if it were called www.joesbowties.com. When thinking about keywords you really want to think about how you expect to be found. What is your particular customer searching for to find you? People aren't going to be searching for Joes Things and if they are, you arguably already own that customer. You want to capture new customers and these people are probably searching for bow ties.

Come up with a list of keywords that you believe your potential customer is searching for. Make sure not to be too generic. You don't have much of a chance for showing up for "ties." That is a very competitive term and not one you should focus on. Generally 3 word keyword combinations are easily targeted and less competitive. Once you have your list of keywords it's time to check out the competition.

Let's take a look at a free tool that is part of Google AdWords. We will visit Google AdWords in detail later in the book, but at this point we are going to focus on one small portion of it. Google AdWords is the paid placement search results that you see at the top and side of Google searches. This advertising coupled with their banner network actually makes up for 96% of Googles revenue. More on that later. Let's skip ahead and signup for a free account at Google AdWords.

Once you have setup your account you can ignore all the prompts to setup a campaign and ads. We will worry about that later. What we want to do is head over to a tool called Keyword Planner. At the time of this writing, it is currently listed under the tools menu from the top of the screen. They tend to change this quite often. From the keyword planner you are going to enter each of your keywords from the list you have generated in the last step. This tool is incredibly powerful and actually shows you the number of times people search for your exact keyword phrase. It is broken down to show searches per month both domestically as well as across the world. You want to make sure you have clicked on the "keyword ideas" tab when you search as opposed to the "ad group ideas" tab. Keyword ideas shows the actual individual keywords people are searching for.

You are going to look at a couple of things. The first thing you want to see is the monthly search volume. Are people searching for what your keyword phrase is? How many times? Is it enough? The next thing you want to look at is the competition. You really would like to consider medium or low competition keywords. Lastly you want to see what dollar amount Google shows as the suggested bid. We are not spending any money at this point but this gives you an idea of what your competition is willing to pay. This shows what they will pay for each click through to their website for this particular keyword. You can get a feel for how expensive the competition is. The less the competition, the less the cost to compete.

What you are ultimately looking for is a keyword phrase with a large search volume coupled with low competition and low bid costs. Once you have reviewed your list, you have probably honed in on one or two winners. These are going to be things that you are going to focus your optimization on. For our example we are going to go with "mens bow ties."

Now that you have decided on a generalized keyword for the overall theme of your site you are going to want to start to build your site and content around this keyword. This means that you want to title your site "Joes Ties - Mens Bow Ties" and use the phrase mens bow ties often and strategically throughout your entire site. Each page of your site should have this keyword phrase once or twice on the page. Your footer or copyright message should be © 2015 Joes Ties | Mens Bow Ties. When writing about your company or your products you should reiterate the exact phrase mens bow ties in addition to your company name. Think of it as a tagline or further clarification to the reader and more importantly relevance to Google. You are making an effort to have your site be considered very relevant for the specific search term Mens Bow Ties without making it look awkward.

Now you have defined your overall keyword for your site. In addition to the main keyword phrase you are going to have many other keyword phrases that you will target for subpages of your site. For example. Say you offered Gucci Mens Bow Ties as one of your options. Presumably you will have a page dedicated to your Gucci ties. On this page you will ensure you are using that specific keyword phrase. Have headings that use the exact phrase on the page and write it into your content on this page. Bold the term where possible.

These keyword phrases on subpages are very important for what we refer to as long tail keywords. Long tail keywords are more detailed searches that people make with 4 or more words in their search. Your subpages ideally will show in the search results. This gives you alternative entry points to your website for people searching the internet. While your home page may not be optimized for Gucci Bow Ties you will want one specific page to be optimized for it and hope that it shows up for that search term.

Content
You may have heard the expression content is king before. I can't stress how true this is. Content really is king. Google is like a giant sponge looking to soak up your unique content to serve it back to people searching. The key to providing good content apart from it being informative is ensuring that it is relevant and unique.

You must write unique content. Google scours the internet 24 hours a day searching for information to make sure they have the most comprehensive search results. When it finds content, it reviews it. If it deems it unique, it indexes it. Indexing means it adds it to its search results. If it is not unique, it merely passes on the information thinking that it already has it indexed from another site. It won't index those pages or show them in any results.

The more content you have, the more potential to be indexed or included in Googles search. Content on your site is an example where it pays to give the whole story. Don't be afraid to write out detailed product descriptions or detailed background information about your company or offering. Regardless of what you are writing about you should be verbose. When writing this content be sure to use keywords for the specific page you are writing about. Less is not more in this case. You want to give the whole love story.

Back to our example on your Gucci Bow Tie page. On this page you should be talking about how your "Gucci Bow Tie offers superior quality compared with other mens bow ties." In this specific sentence we were able to work in our general site keyword phrase in addition to the specific pages keyword phrase.

A good rule of thumb is that you want to have your keyword phrase appear in more than 1% of the words on the page. If you are writing a summary that is 500 words then you should have your keyword phrase mentioned at least 5 times. Additionally as a rough rule of thumb a good solid page has at least 300 words. Not every page can have this much content but a blog or about us page should shoot for a minimum of 300 words. The longer the better.

Images
Images are an often overlooked opportunity to add relevance to search engines and bring additional traffic to your site. All images on your site, regardless of where they are being used, should be saved with relevant names. What I'm referring to is the actual image name. For example the image that you have on your computer currently named DSC059648.jpg is useless if added to your site like that.

You should rename this image to what it is related to. Assume this image was of a gucci bow tie. You should name the file

gucci-bow-tie-red-and-green.jpg

Put dashes in between the words and include the brand or details about the product. Google as well as Bing and others show images in many of their search results like the one shown below.

The images shown above are actually free advertising.
You are not paying anything for clicks through those
pictures unlike the product placements on the right or ads
along the top. Those pictures are showing up there
because they are named appropriately and google then
decides they are relevant. The beauty is that these
images are direct links into your website. This is the
easiest way to get additional free traffic.

It doesn't stop there though. While Google looks at the
actual name of the file they also look at the ALT tags. ALT
tags are the words that describe an image that you can
see if the image fails to load or is slow to load. Sometime
you will see the alt message in its place while the full
image actually loads.

These ALT tags are easily edited through WordPress or
Shopify or almost all of the major ecommerce platforms
you will be using. Make the ALT tags relevant to the page
you are adding it to. Use the same keyword phrase. "Red
and Green Gucci Bow Tie." All of these factors add
relevance in Googles mind to build the case that your page
is relevant to people's searches.

When getting your product images together to use on the
site I believe strongly that consistency can differentiate
your from your competitors. I don't like the sloppy look of
mis-sized images with different backgrounds. You may not
be a Photoshop wizard but there are a number of simple
image editing tools online as well as built into many of the
online ecommerce platforms.

If you don't want to bother doing the photo editing yourself
I would recommend a service called Remove the
Background. Remove the background does exactly as it
states. You upload your images and define the specific
dimensions you want the image returned in and how much
padding you would like around the image. For about $1.25
an image, they will return your images in a couple of days
without a background and perfectly sized and cropped like
your other images. Its a great service that can save you a
bunch of time and help you stand out from the less
professional looking sites.

Meta Tags
Meta tags refer to items that appear in the code but are not
necessarily visible to the user when they are on your page.
In the early days of the internet you could use the tag

called Meta-Keywords and load it up with keywords that you wanted your page to be found for in search. The search engines would use this information to classify and show your site.

People started gaming this system and adding lots of keywords and ones that weren't relevant for the content. Needless to say meta-keywords are all but dead. They are not used by most search engines and unnecessary. Search engines now are able to read the content of your site and automatically define relevant keywords and list the frequency in which the keywords appear to generate a more accurate keyword list for your site.

While meta keywords are not given any priority, the meta description is an exception. The meta description is the summary that appears below any link in google. Referring to the image above and looking at the last search result which is Neiman Marcus, the meta description is "Free shipping and free returns always on Gucci Tuxedo Bow Tie.." Note how they have strategically included the same keyword phrase in the description.

You want to write a unique description for each page. Many sites will auto fill your meta description with the first couple of sentences from your page. Don't be lazy. Replace this with a unique summary no longer than 160 characters. Make sure to use the intended keyword phrase in your description. Don't copy and paste the description from content that you have already written on your page.

If you stay focused on making your pages full of content and using the relevant keywords, image tags, headings, titles and descriptions you have laid the groundwork for your onsite search engine optimization. This is just as important as future marketing and off-site SEO techniques we will discuss later.

Launching

An often overlooked part of officially opening your business is the actual opening event. There will be plenty of time for you to make up events in the future. You will struggle coming up with news to tell people, but why struggle when there actually is something to talk about. Launching is a big deal and something you should both be proud of and something you want to tell everyone about.

The first step in launching is defining a date. You must put a line in the sand and hold yourself to a date. Without a planned launch date, time will come and go and you will find countless reasons to delay the launch of your site. You need to come to grips with the fact that you are not going to have everything perfect.

There is no such thing as perfect and your site will always be changing. Your work and progress doesn't stop after you launch. Just the opposite. Your work actually begins when you launch. You will be changing content, making updates, revising layouts, etc., etc. You only get one chance to make a first impression to your friends and family however there comes a time when you must launch. If you are feeling uncomfortable, this is natural. You have spent countless hours and work to get to this point and you don't know how it is going to be received. But don't let this keep you from moving forward. LAUNCH already..

"How do I effectively launch," you say. Let's discuss this further. One of the first steps of starting your business from our list of to-dos was to compile a list of everyone you know. This ultimately is going to be a list of email addresses. This is your one chance to reach out to those random people you haven't spoken to in years. Collect all of these lists. Go into your old AOL account and gather up the oldies and goodies. You also should have been collecting email addresses from your landing page that you have been sending people while you built your full site. All of these should be added to your email software awaiting your launch day.

While your landing page should help build the hype you need to also start seeding your social network sites a month or two before you launch as well. But wait you say, "I don't have social network sites or even know what you are talking about." No problem. It's time to get social. While you may have ignored social before, it is time to embrace it. Tweeting is no longer just for the birds. We will discuss each of the different social sites later in the book but for now let's assume you have at least a Facebook account. If you don't, it's time to sign up for one. Succumb to the power of Facebook and realize that it has incredible reach.

Starting a month or so before your launch, you should post some coming soon images and a brief message as to what you are working on. You don't want to tell too much. The secrecy helps build the hype. "It's Coming. Wait For It" or "Company Name - Coming Soon..." You want to engage but not tell all. Link to your landing page and encourage everyone to register to be notified and receive a special offer when you launch. Do this a couple of times but not too many that you are going to annoy people. During this time you should also be friending everyone in the world. Your sisters' friends dog groomer. Perfect. Friend request sent. Your brother-in-laws boss. Perfect. Friend request sent.

During this time you will work on an opening email blast. You would like to do something catchy that looks professional. Most of the email providers have pre made templates that do a great job of handling the basics but you probably want a customized image to include in your initial launch. This is something you should consider using Fiverr or Canva for. Fiverr is the site we discussed when coming up with your logo.

The other alternative is a web based program called Canva. Canva helps a beginner upload a image or use their stock photos for $1 and dress up your images with professional looking images. This is a great tool to create your own professional quality images. You don't have to know how to use Photoshop or advanced graphic design programs. It does take a little getting used to but can save you a lot of money. When making your email image make smaller versions to use on your social sites as well.

Lastly before launching you want to create a special coupon code. This coupon code is for friends and family (or anyone who cares to be honest.) You are going to offer your opening coupon code or free giveaway for a set amount of time and possibly even for a set number of people. People follow some basic social signals and it is important to pull these emotional strings. You must show scarcity and urgency. An expiring offer with an exclusive offer just for friends and family does just that.

The time has come and you are ready to open your store. You have set the date and posted a couple of times socially to build hype. You have compiled an email list of everyone you can think of. You have made sure your launch day isn't a long holiday weekend and that people are around. You have made some initial launch graphics and an email campaign to be sent. You have read through your site for grammatical errors and the time is now. Open your site and let's do this.

Send out your email campaign in the wee hours of the day you are launching. Most people read their email early in the morning and you want to be included in that time. Second you need to post to all of your social networks. Instagram, Twitter, Facebook, Etc., Etc. We will discuss these in more detail later but now is the time to post. Share your friends and family discount. You should make your friends and family email personal and ask them to share it with anyone they want. The more the merrier. Don't be concerned about giving out the discount to too many people. 100% of $0 is zero and you don't want that. It's better to make sales and break even just to get your name and site out there. At this point you will take anything you can get.

Inexpensive Tools to Look Big

When the internet and online commerce were in their infancy, the cost of starting a new company was steep. You would hire a web development company or maybe a freelancer and ultimately end up with an acceptable solution but one that probably lacked most of the functionality you were looking for.

Fast forward 15 years or so and things have evolved. Internet speeds have greatly increased and thousands of new companies have sprung up and evolved to offer highly targeted services for micro niches related to selling online. These tools allow you to easily do things that would have taken weeks and thousands of dollars in the past. You now have the ability to compete with larger companies by using similar tools at a fraction of the cost.

We mention many of these services throughout the book but have compiled a list below to organize them for you in one spot. To get a simple linkable list with 50 resources including these, you can find it at

http://longlivetheinternet.com/book-gift.

We have compiled a simple file that you download to your computer with links to all these resources.

Some of these services are better than others but this is a list of all services that we have personally used and can attest to. They help make your life simpler and fill very specific needs. Full disclaimer some of these links are affiliate links and we may make a dollar or two if you click on the link and signup with them. We greatly appreciate it.

Domain Name
GoDaddy - One of the cheaper options and easy to use. GoDaddy is where you will register your domain name. YOURWEBSITE.COM

Logo
99Designs - This site lets you hold a mini contest for your logo design. Hundreds of people submit their logo concepts based on your directions and you ultimately pick and award a winner.
Pixellogo - Offering thousands of beautiful logos to choose from you get the raw files and can easily modify them to suit your name and needs and the cost is about $30 to $40.
Fivver - A site where thousands of people from all over the world are willing to do tasks such as logo design to video production for $5. This is a treasure trove of resources.

Contracts
Legal Zoom - If you are looking for boilerplate legal agreements that you can trust you can get them here. From standard purchase agreements to partnership documents, Legal Zoom offers a simple solution for contracts. Save hundreds of dollars on legal fees.

Hosting

BlueHost - One of the cheapest reliable hosting solutions for a WordPress site or other basic sites that you may be hosting. Easily have a Wordpress site up and hosted for $5 a month.

Host Gator - Another affordable hosting solution that is user friendly and customer service oriented.

Email

Google Apps - The most powerful email and online business suite available. At $5 a month a user you won't find a better solution.

GoDaddy - When purchasing your domain name you may decide to just get email through GoDaddy. Its inferior to Google Apps but may make your setup one step easier.

Faxes

eFax - The leader in the space eFax lets you setup a fax number and receive all your faxes as scanned pdf files to your email inbox. You can also send faxes by emailing attachments to an email address.

Task Managing

Trello - This online solution is free and lets you create boards for organizing your daily tasks and projects.

Basecamp - This is a more involved solution to project management and really designed for companies coordinating with other companies but a solid solution if you are managing larger teams of people.

Ecommerce Platforms

Shopify - Our ecommerce platform of choice because of the ease, customization capabilities and third party eco-system of third party add-ons. This is our recommendation for you.

Volusion - This is a more expensive solution that we don't believe is as user friendly for beginners but has a huge following and is a viable solution that thousands of users love.

Square Space - This is a beautiful solution with sexy looking sites but search engine optimization is not their strength. Many of the things you should be able to do to make your site more visible are not available here.

Images

Canva - This lets you be a graphic designer by using pre-designed templates and layouts. It is free if you don't pay for their stock photography and an incredible tool to make your site and social sharing images professional looking.

Flickr - This is owned by Yahoo and a repository of millions of images online. You can search for stock images that you are allowed to use commercially for free.

Unsplash - This site posts one image a day of beautifully shot scenes that are royalty free and you can use in your advertising or site design. Doesn't have the depth of Flickr and you can't search the images but they have beautiful shots.

Favicon Generator - A favicon is the little image that shows in the top of the browser when you are on your website. Its a tiny little icon. This site lets you upload your logo or image of choice and converts it to a favicon so you can upload it to your site to replace the default one.

Tiny PNG - This site lets you upload any of your png files for free and it will smush them down in size to increase your website loading time. It will reduces the size of your png images about 30% on average without decreasing the quality of the picture. It's magic.

Email Marketing

Mailchimp - Our choice for email advertising and list building for beginners. Simple drag and drop tools and a clean easy layout makes it our beginners' choice.

Constant Contact - The leader in the space, Constant Contact offers all the same features as Mailchimp and just as reliably. It is just not as user friendly from a user interface perspective.

AWeber - This is our choice if you are building your own site and hosting outside of one of the e commerce platforms available. They are very reliable and have incredible drip email campaign tools.

Phone

Google Voice - A free solution to get a business number to route to your phone and also transcribe your voicemail into an email.

Grasshopper - This is an easy to use phone system that lets you setup a phone tree and forwarding to multiple phones and various people. It is a simple self-service phone system that lets you look like a big company inexpensively.

RingCentral - This is another option and competitor to Grasshopper. They have a great app that comes with their plans that lets you make outgoing calls from your new vanity phone number so you can call from your 800 number etc.

One Box - This is similar to both Grasshopper and Ring Central and very easy to use. Owned by the same company as eFax, it offers many of the same features as the other two phone services. We have used all of these services and they are pretty much the same but each offers different phone numbers. If you are looking for a particular area code you may need to check each out.

E-Signatures

Sign In Blue - Full disclaimer that we built Sign In Blue so we are biased here. I will tell you upfront this is not the most robust solution on the market and if you are a super advanced user there are other options out there. However, if you are looking for a simple, easy to use, e-signature solution that is what Sign In Blue can offer you.

Storage

Dropbox - The single best recommendation we can make is to sign up for a Dropbox account now. It is free and incredible. Without getting too technical, Dropbox lets you have a folder on your computer that is automatically backed up to the internet and available online at your account and any other computer you install it on. For example you have a folder of pictures on your computer. Merely dragging new folders into that folder will upload them to the internet and download them to other computers you have. Never fear losing files again and you are able to easily share files across computers.

Box.com - Not as cool as Dropbox, box.com is a little more corporate in nature. Its acts similarly to Dropbox although not as effortlessly but allows you to set more restrictions on the files for sharing. You can share files with coworkers and put expiration dates and track file downloads. It is a more complicated solution than Dropbox but if you are a larger operation it may make sense. It is not cheap though.

Google Drive - Part of Google Apps you actually get storage space within the Google ecosystem. If you have a Gmail account you are able to save your attachments directly into Google Drive. It is convenient from that perspective but in our opinion doesn't complete with Dropbox.

Traffic Analysis
Webmaster Tools - One of the most important tools to make sure your website is configured properly and performing as best as it can for search engines is Google Webmaster Tools. This free tool from Google provides insight into what sites are linking to your site, what pages of your site are indexed in Googles search and how you can improve your site to please Google.

Google Analytics - This is probably our most entertaining tool and one that every online site should be using. Google Analytics is also free and is an incredibly powerful traffic analysis tool. Amongst hundreds of other statistical points you have access to these types of data points. Number of visits, referring sites, and time spent on site, geographical breakdown of site visitors, entry pages and exit pages, sales conversions and how they came into your site, bounce rate, number of pages viewed, frequency of visits, and real time (creepy) stats of people on your site at any time and what they are looking at. Its amazing and free.

SEO

Moz - If you are looking for more advanced search engine optimization tools then Moz is one of the leaders in this space. They have an incredible free blog which is chock full of educational articles about SEO. Their service is not cheap but lets you monitor and track progress of your rankings for particular keywords week after week. If you are making a formal SEO push for particular terms it may make sense for you to try Moz. They also offer a great free tool called Open Site Explorer which lets you research the backlinks of competitors' sites to see where there may be an opportunity for you to get links as well.

Ahrefs - A competitor to Moz, ahrefs offers a similar product to Moz which is very powerful for tracking the progress of your search engine campaigns. I find the backlink checker and reports more accurate and more detailed at Ahrefs but other than that they are competitive solutions.

Marketing Email Automation

GetDrip - This is a great tool for easily adding a popup to your website and having people opt into a timed email sequence. While you can implement this by yourself with your MailChimp or constant contact or AWeber account, getDrip has been designed specifically for this purpose. They actually will help you draft your email campaign and setup the popup on your site. Interesting fact is that after testing thousands of calls to action they have determined that adding crash course to the end of your title has a substantially higher opt-in rate. Ex 7-day GPS Tracking Crash Course.

Advertising

AdWords - The secret behind Googles piles of cash, AdWords lets you bid to have your site show in their search results based on what users search for. If you can't organically rank for the terms you want to show up for you can pay for it. How much are you willing to pay for each click through to your site? An incredibly powerful advertising tool for your website allowing you to laser focus advertising dollars on people showing intent for specific keywords you define. Its self-service and can take some time to setup but it is worth it.

Bing Ads - A complete knock off of Google AdWords, Bing offers a cost per click tool as well. Their pay for keyword search results also feeds to Yahoo and you can sometimes get a cheaper cpc then on Google. The good news with Bing is that once you have fine-tuned and configured your AdWords campaign you can easily export the settings and import them into a new campaign at Bing.

Facebook Ads - One of the newer advertising platforms Facebook continues to refine their capabilities for advertising but with their latest upgrade you are able to focus your ads and define where, who, and how much you are willing to spend for your ads. Similar to AdWords you don't have to pay if your ad isn't clicked on. The addition of income brackets and Facebook interest targeting makes it a powerful tool for targeting potential customers.

Amazon Ads- Already the largest retailer online, Amazon doesn't want to leave any stone unturned. Apart from potentially selling your products online at Amazon, they offer and advertising platform to show your products in search queries where they may not have a matching product in their expansive catalog. While we are honestly the least experienced with this particular advertising avenue, I think there is substantial potential to pick up some customers from some more obscure offerings for a relatively cheap cost of acquisition. It is worth a further look.

Yahoo Ads - Still one of the largest content providers online, Yahoo has an incredible amount of traffic on their site. While they made a deal with Bing to power their keyword search results, they have made an active push over the last year or so to increase revenues streams for the company through small business advertising platforms. It has flown mostly under the radar but you can actually get quite a bit of exposure inexpensively through Yahoos new Gemini ad program. You don't have to pay for impressions and can also pay for performance only. You would be surprised at the amount of exposure you can get for small budgets. I would recommend you experiment with Yahoo.

Pinterest - One of the latest platforms to release advertising for small businesses is Pinterest. While they are currently touting Promoted Pins as a secret invite only feature, anyone can sign up. You basically pay for the amount you are willing to pay when someone clicks on one of your pins which takes them to your site. This is a great outlet for advertising. You only pay for clicks and not repins or likes and views. Furthermore, when someone clicks on the link they have actually already seen the product you are showing them. Their intent is great. Their platform is still a little clunky but they should work that out over time.

Social Posting

Hootsuite - This allows you to pre-schedule your tweets in advance. You can enter them and set the time of day and day that you would like them shared. You can configure how many times to share it and gives you the ability to automate a lot of your tweeting work.

Buffer - Another option to manage your social media posts and statistics. Buffer is an easy way to track what is working and what is not.

IFTTT - The acronym for "If This Then That" this service allows you to setup automated procedures or recipes as they call them. This service lets you perform some amazing tasks for free that are triggered by other events. An example is to share all your Facebook posts on to twitter. Another is to download all images posted on your Instagram feed to your Dropbox account.

Google Alerts - This allows you to setup a notification. Either daily or weekly or in real time you can be notified at no cost for mentions of your brand or name online. Google Alerts lets you enter whatever terms you want. It will then scour the internet and any mentions of your brand or name will be emailed to you with a link to the post.

Outsourcing

Fiverr - This site lets you shop through thousands of different services from people online mostly from developing countries for $5.

Printing

Moo - Beautiful business cards or printed materials. A step above all the cheap online solutions that offer free cards. You get what you pay for.

Supplies

Amazon - It seems crazy but sometimes it is actually less expensive to order office supplies online then to get them at the local office supply store. Look at the amazing office supply prices amazon has. You will be surprised.

Consult This

We discussed the lack of importance that we feel a business plan offers. Secondary to business plans but also somewhat of a waste are consultants. Consultants and expensive brand and strategy companies are inappropriate for small startup companies. I'm not saying that these professionals don't have value. In fact the complete opposite. They have incredible value and years of experience. If you want to speak with them and use them though, it is going to cost you. This cost is not something you can afford when getting started.

The good news is that you are reading this book. At a fraction of the cost of big fancy consultants, you are getting the knowledge and experience of many failed and successful ventures. The lessons you learn are based on many, many projects and hopefully will save you countless hours. In addition to published e-books like this, google offers instant access to hundreds of bloggers and chat forums offering incredible advice from real professionals.

The amount of free information has never been more accessible. From YouTube tutorials to detailed setup walkthroughs for just about any service, it is all one search away. All it takes is patience and time to read through them. Below are sites and resources that I think are valuable from people that I think have an incredible amount to share? This by no means is a comprehensive list and there are countess free resources available.

KiSS Metrics - www.kissmetrics.com

Smart Passive Income Patt Flynn - www.smartpassiveincome.com

MOZ - www.moz.com

Bootstrapping Ecommerce - www.bootstrappingecommerce.com

Entrepreneur - www.entrepreneur.com

Practical Ecommerce - www.practicalecommerce.com

Allocation of Funds

While we aren't going to dive into detailed accounting and bookkeeping, it is important for you to keep an eye on your funds. When starting a new ecommerce site with a limited budget, every little bit matters. We talked briefly about QuickBooks and how we think it is a great option for your bookkeeping. Apart from bookkeeping though, you need to manage your cash flow tightly. What happens when you start selling? What are you going to re-order? What expenses do you have? Do you have any money for advertising? Try and budget and account for your money in advance instead of spending everything you have the moment you have it.

Your business will be a living creature and cash flow will constantly swing back and forth but if you plan ahead, you can keep your unforeseen expenses from putting you in a bind. Are you prepared for the holidays? Are you going to have enough inventory when sales pick up? Don't wait until it is too late to re-order and miss the busy shopping season. On the flip side don't order 10 of everything. The beauty of ecommerce is nobody actually knows how many of each item you have in stock. Get 1 of each item and restock it once you sell it. It can make your selection look larger and keep you from tying up all your money in inventory. If it is selling well, then increase your quantity.

In summary you need to watch each and every expense and nothing should be too large that it accounts for more than 20% of your available funds. If you are buying from multiple suppliers then evenly distribute amongst them. When starting out, look for vendors that have low minimum orders. See if they will extend net 30 terms or maybe even entertain consignment. When sourcing for office materials, packing materials, or packaging, source online. You can always find things cheaper online than going to your neighborhood store. Like we said earlier, look here at the amazon office section. You would be surprised it may be cheaper to order online and have it mailed to you than actually picking it up at a store.

[3]
Marketing and Off Site SEO

Monitoring your traffic

ONE OF THE MOST important things you will do when setting up your online store is to install Google Analytics. Google Analytics is the most powerful tool you will have access to and best of all its free. Your first step is to visit the site and create a new account. You will be given a small snippet of code to install on your site. You will either give it to the person working on your website or you will find in your shopping cart software where to insert the code. Most shopping software providers now provide and easy way for you to insert the tracking code. Its the most widely used analytical tracking tool and a quick google search for "inserting Google Analytics code in Shopify" or whatever your shopping platform or website platform is will give you step by step instructions.

Once you have signed up for the account, inserted your tracking tag and verified your ownership of the site, the fun part begins. Google Analytics is actually a website traffic analysis tool. What does that mean you say? Google Analytics tracks all traffic to and from and all pages viewed while on your website. It shares with you where people are located in the world down to the city, how they found your site, how long they were on the site and thousands and thousands of other data points that are priceless when trying to improve your business. Find out what messages are working and what pages are forcing people to leave. You can see which keywords are sending traffic to your site and in real time you can see people on your website and the pages they are looking at.

Once you have played around with Google Analytics and learnt the basics, you will want to create a conversion goal. A conversion goal is a goal that you would like your visitors to complete. For example you would like to track every sale on your website so you would create a goal of purchasing an item. This can be a little tricky but don't get discouraged. You really need to complete this portion as this information is priceless. What you are doing is laying the groundwork to be able to track where each and every sale came from. This becomes incredibly powerful when trying to assess the value of your marketing spend.

Once your conversion tracking is in place and collecting data, you can accurately see the source of each and every sale. For example, someone searched on Google for Blue Monkey and found your site and then was on your site for

5 minutes and ultimately purchased. You can also use this tool to see what doesn't work. Let's say you were paying to advertise on a local organization site or some other website. Maybe they told you it was a great idea to spend $100 to have your banner ad on their site for a month because they get 1 million visitors. Well, with Google Analytics you can see in black and white if any of the traffic from that banner ad converts to sales and more importantly how much traffic you received in total over the course of your month.

Let's assume you had 4 clicks and visits from the site you were advertising on. Take your $100 and divide it by the 4 people that visited your site through this link. That is $25 per visitor. Does that make sense for you? Probably not, but maybe it does. You see this at least gives you the tools to help make those decisions. If you are using other forms of advertising and getting a comparable conversion rate but only paying 50 cents for each visitor then clearly this is a better source for you. The key is finding the cheapest source of qualified traffic.

Let's discuss qualified traffic further. Traffic is key but only if it is the right traffic. That is not to say you don't love any traffic because traffic is traffic. But if you are paying for the traffic then you need to make sure they are converting. Converting can mean different things for different people. It really depends on what you are looking to have your visitors do. Maybe you only want them to sign up for your newsletter and this is a valuable conversion for you. Maybe you want an actual purchase. This is what you need to be able to assess. What does it cost to acquire a sale or conversion? Furthermore is it profitable. If you are paying $20 in advertising for every conversion but the average conversion is resulting in $10 net to you, you are actually losing money on each sale.

You must review these numbers and constantly monitor the traffic to your site. This traffic, its source, cost, and behavior is the lifeblood of your site. Don't be afraid or turned off by this. Numbers don't lie. As long as you can find avenues of traffic that convert to sales and cost less than the profit you make from them, you have a sustainable business. If you can't then at least you can isolate what's not working to focus on alternate traffic sources. I can't stress the importance of this enough. Read this section again if you need to but your profitability lies in your cost of sale.

Who is sending you what traffic? Webmaster Tools

Now that you have setup Google Analytics and you are able to monitor the traffic on your site, let's move on to the next step. Google Webmaster Tools is the next thing you will want to setup on your site. Similar to Google Analytics you will need to insert a line of code into your site to claim ownership of the site. Once claimed, Webmaster Tools will take a couple days to populate with the pertinent information for your site. Webmaster Tools is a little more detailed than Google Analytics but is the backbone for your SEO or search engine marketing campaign.

Webmaster Tools provides insight into how Google views your website. They will show you the keyword frequency of your site. This helps to make sure your content is aligned with what you would like to show up for in searches. You will also be able to see any errors with your site as well as other websites that are linking to you.

Google offers the most reliable and comprehensive search because of their state-of-the-art algorithm. This coupled with the fact that they have millions of servers veraciously hunting for new content and information online, keeps them ahead. Once these servers find this information, they "index" it or add it to their search results. This allows you to see who is linking to your site and is known as a backlink. You want to ensure you site is indexed and showing in Googles results and this is what Webmaster Tools is for.

Webmaster Tools will alert you to any broken links on your site or other content or pages that are not showing properly. Additionally it will show you best practices to ensure you are displaying your content the best that you can. Play by Googles rules and you will be rewarded with traffic from their search.

You have made it this far. Good work. The good news is that you have setup the initial tools you need to effectively manage your advertising and marketing efforts online. Now its time to actually dig in and put some of these monitoring tools to work. If you haven't gone through those setup stages then it becomes difficult to measure the effectiveness of the time and money you are expending.

AdWords

The flagship of Googles holdings, Google AdWords is what makes up for roughly 68% of their annual revenue as of 2014 numbers. What is AdWords you say? It's how Google makes their money. Have you ever searched for something on google and seen a more prominent result at the top and right portion of the page like you see below.

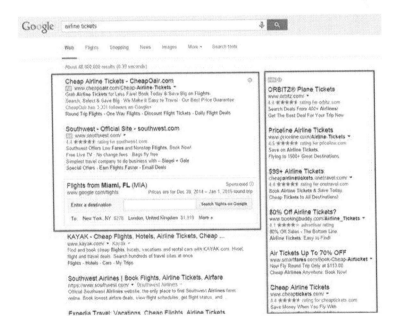

Those portions in red above are actually all advertisements. These are paid placements from companies vying for your attention and ultimately your traffic. But this space is not just for huge Fortune 500

companies with enormous marketing budgets. Google has built a robust ad placement tool they call Google AdWords that allows everyone to compete on equal grounds for the same market and customers clicks.

Let's discuss this a little further. Google charges you on a CPC basis. CPC stands for cost per click and means that you only pay when someone actually clicks on the link. This is different than paying to merely show your ad. The original online advertising model was based on CPM. CPM refers to a cost per 1000 impressions. As people got more sophisticated and comfortable online they started tuning out display banner ads. This means that the effectiveness of these ads decreased and people were less willing to pay just to have their ad shown to people. The beauty of a CPC model is that if the visitor isn't clicking to come to your site then you are not being charged.

So how exactly do you determine your CPC for various keywords and what you should be paying for each click? Well it's not so simple. Google shows your ads based on a number of factors. First and most important is the amount of money that you are willing to pay for a click. If you are willing to pay $2.00 per click than you are going to show higher than those willing to pay 50 cents for each click. This can be confusing but in summary, the more you are willing the pay, the higher your ad results are going to show. I want to reiterate that we are discussing only the ad portions I pointed out earlier in the search results. There are two portions of any Google search. There is paid advertising placement and there is organic results which are free placement. We are only discussing the paid placements at this time.

Let's talk now about setting up your Google AdWords campaign. When starting a campaign on Google you will need to come up with a list of keywords or search terms that you believe people would be searching for to find your site. It is best to start with highly specific keywords and work your way out from there. Google has millions and millions of searches a day and you can be highly selective with your terms. The more highly targeted your search string, the more likely the person clicking on it, is a potential customer for you.

For example let's assume you are selling Easter Egg Necklaces. Ideally you would start with the exact keyword of "East Egg Necklaces" and then build a list from there. Alternatively "Easter necklaces" would be another good keyword. You want to be careful not to use terms that are too broad. For example "necklaces" while still relevant is too broad. The likelihood that someone searching for "necklaces" is interested in an Easter egg necklace is far less than someone searching for "Easter necklaces." You really want to laser your focus in. You can always broaden your keywords later if you have too narrow of a market defined.

When setting up your campaign there are a couple of things you want to consider and make sure you address. I can tell you from many wasted dollars and lots of aggravation that I wish I had been told these two tips before I started with Google AdWords. Google would prefer you not know these things which is why they burry these options deep and set them by default to benefit Google.

Tip 1

When creating a keyword campaign and adding a keyword there are 3 types of matching that can be used. They won't ask you when adding the keywords but you need to make sure to edit the match type accordingly. I believe strongly in using exact match and then adding the specific keyword terms that I want targeted. This may take a little more work up front coming up with all the potential keywords but can save you substantial wasted funds.

> Broad Match - This match type contains your keywords in any order and may include other keywords. For example "I hate Easter and necklaces" would result in your ad showing and

clearly is not someone you would like to pay for to visit your site.

Exact Match - The exact match contains only your keywords and specifically in the order you have entered them. It can result in leaving some other terms out indiscriminately but further refining it later and reviewing Googles opportunity recommendations will ultimately provide you with all the potential keywords you want. "Easter Necklaces" is what your ad will show for.

Phrase Match - Phrase match contains all the words in order but may include other words before or after your phrase. Unfortunately this means if someone is searching "free Easter necklaces" you will show up in the search and this may not be someone willing to purchase once they click through to your site.

Tip 2

The second tip and another one that Google rather you not change is limiting your search results to just the google network. By default your campaign will be set to run on all search partners. I have found the search partner to provide often suspiciously less engaged visitors to the site.

Google offers a revenue share program with search partners like AVG antivirus and other companies where they share the amount you are willing to pay for the click with the search originator. It is in these companies best interest to have users click on the terms regardless of whether they are relevant or not.

This is a huge market and not one that I'm saying you have to forget all together. They just tend to show a higher bounce rate (leave your website without reading or going deeper into your site) than normal Google search leads.

Your first step will be to change your campaign settings to "Search Network Only" and then you will want to find the option where it defines "Networks." Edit this and make sure that search partners is disabled. This will prevent your keyword ads from running on other sites that often produce less favorable results.

If you have a highly targeted list of keywords though and are finding that you are not able to produce enough traffic at the price you are willing to pay, solely through Google search results, then you can consider using the search partners. I would recommend that you setup an additional campaign inclusive of search partners though and have a reduced CPC set for that campaign. Maybe you are willing to pay 60 cents for clicks from Google directly but only 25 cents for clicks from a search partner. This lets you capture some of the volume of these additional searches but at a lower cost with the understanding that they are potentially less engaged visitors.

Additional Notes of Interest
Google AdWords has an incredible list of features, from Geographic targeting, to retargeting visitors that have been to your site with banner ads created by Googles ad maker.

You really should take the time and browse through the different options available to you. Further refining your campaigns is only going to help you become more profitable.

You can ensure that you are not wasting money on the wrong demographic. If your product is only relevant on the east coast of the US then limit your keyword results to that geographic local. If you believe that your potential customer is not searching on a mobile phone then limit your targeting to desktops and tablets.

There are incredible features to let you fine tune your market. Take the time and learn them and it will pay off. You don't have to do it all at once. I like to take a look and tinker with it once a month once you have your initial settings configured. You can't spend more than a half an hour or so each time you work with it or you will go crazy. Refine it over time.

Emails

In order to ensure that emails are properly delivered and to nicely track details like opens and click throughs, you are going want to send emails from an established email provider. Countless studies have shown time and time again that Email marketing is by far the highest return on capital compared to all other marketing options. The time to start building your email list is now. It doesn't matter whether you are starting with 2 email addresses or hundreds, you need to start building your list now. It may seem daunting at first and silly to only have a list of 5 or 10 people but you have to start somewhere.

Building your email list doesn't mean you start a spreadsheet on your computer and start adding names to it. You are going to need to get organized and add them somewhere where you can manage them. Nowadays you can't send an email from your personal account to a large group of people and expect it to get delivered. Personal email account are designed just for that. Personal email. You need to use a professional email delivery service. This doesn't mean though that you need to pay. There is quite a lot of competition in this space and there are lots of good options on the market now. The space has gotten so competitive that many of the bells and whistles that were only offered by certain companies have been adopted by all of them. The three big ones that I can recommend are the following.

Mail Chimp - Clean, simple, and easy to use. They have a free account and it has an incredible amount of options and functionality for a free account. Caveat is, as you grow they will want some money for the service. Once you get over 2000 subscribers you will need to pay them but you have a while to go. If you are using Shopify they offer an app called Chimpify which ties directly into your software for seamless subscriptions to your email list when orders are place.

AWeber - This is an incredible robust option and one that I recommend for anyone selling ebooks or other digital products. They have an amazing system for scheduling a sequence of follow up emails to slowly convert your subscribers to purchasers. We use this for some of our subscription sites and more involved sales process sites. Love them.

Constant Contact - Probably the largest of the three constant contact has been around since the beginning. They have broad appeal and substantial name recognition from TV commercials. They offer all the same features as the others. You can't go wrong with them.

Once you have decided on your provider and setup an account you will create a list. This list is where you will begin to add all of your subscribers. If you have an initial list that you were keeping on a spreadsheet or word doc you can paste or import all of these into the software. Once they are on the list you will begin to build your list from here. The beauty of these systems is they will handle the subscribing and unsubscribing for you. When people want to be added or removed from the list they have many different ways for you to automate the process and incorporate into your site.

> **> WARNING <**
>
> While it may be tempting to import large lists you have collected from other sources and add them to your list, beware. Each of these providers take their services seriously and you must confirm that the people have agreed to receive email from you when adding them. If you receive too many spam complaints, your account may be frozen and you may be prevented from sending emails.

There is a balance to adding people to your list and getting their permission. Many of the email companies incorporate 2 step confirmation. This means that once someone signs up for your newsletter or email list, they will receive an email to opt-in. If they don't click on the link in that email to confirm their subscription, they will not be added. While this does ensure people want to actually receive your emails, it also reduces the number of subscribers you will get. Its a balance of too little or too much but ultimately if you stay the course and diligently collect emails at special events or shows and online through your site, your list will grow.

Once you have your list and you are starting to grow your subscribers, I would recommend that you build a basic template for all of your emails. Each of these programs come with email design systems and most of them handle responsive email so that it ensures your emails will look good on a mobile device and computer. Once you have your default template defined, you are then able to change out images or messages rather easily without having to start from scratch each time you send an email. You will copy over the template and modify what you already had.

Emailing is something that you need to be diligent about. It is not quick and can take time and many people therefore decide it is not important. This is wrong and you need to commit yourself to emailing. Keep things fresh and keep them regular. If you want to email once a month then stick with it. If you are more adventurous and committed and want to send bi weekly, weekly or even daily than go for it.

Consistency though is what will win over time. A sporadic email whenever you feel like it is far less effective than slow and steady emails over time. Some buyers will need to see your brand and become comfortable with it over time. This comfort may not come from their first visit to your site, but may come after receiving a half a dozen emails. Everyone is different.

Don't underestimate email. It's important.

Blogging

Oh the dreaded blogging. "What in the world am I going to talk about," you say as you sit down to write your first blog. The good news is, initially it doesn't really matter. The beauty of blogging is that every little bit helps and the more you write the better you will be. There are two types of blogging that I want to touch on and two sets of beliefs in this space.

The first question you need to ask yourself is whether your site is a blog first and foremost. Are you building a blog that happens to offer products or services for sale? On the flip side, are you an ecommerce site primarily? Are you looking to just get some traffic by blogging on your ecommerce site? This question will dictate largely how you write and the time you commit to blogging.

If you are going to be a blogger officially and your posts are the meat and potatoes of your site then you need to plan out your blogs more thoroughly. You have to create a voice for yourself and think about what your readers or potential readers want to read about. You need to make a connection with your readers and draw them back to your content on a regular basis. I am far less qualified to advise you on this front and there are many amazing bloggers with large followings that can advise on this front.

The latter option is that of content created for sites primarily intended to sell products or items online. This is done from driving interested parties to your site and then having them find you indirectly. We have talked a bit about paid advertising and marketing efforts but let's look at blogging to generate search engine bait. Google loves content and relevant content to your site is what is going to continue to bring new users to your site without having to pay for them.

When you create new content and write blog posts, Google will index your site and find that new content. Hopefully your content is rich with the relevant keywords you are targeting and in return when people search online for these keywords your blog posts will eventually show in the results. Each page or blog post that you create is an additional page indexed in the search engines. This is where you are looking to find additional web surfers and bring them to your site.

But where do I start you think? Don't over think it. Writing is largely about throwing down words on the paper and continuing to shape them together. I'm not the best writer but you can't get better without trying. Without trying, you are sure to produce no content. Think about telling a story or explaining one of your products. Maybe you will write a seasonal piece about holidays or what's happening in your area or industry. Do a product review. Think about your target customer and write about what interests them. It doesn't have to be directly about your products. As long as it is somewhat related and appealing to your customer then it's worthwhile.

For example say you are selling auto parts online. Chances are that your customer is potentially a man who repairs his own car or works on cars. Writing a blog post on the newest cars that were shown at the recent auto show with pictures is a great piece of content. You don't have to have gone to the show to write about it. There are hundreds of other people who have done that for you. Google it and find the stories and write your own piece about the show with pictures. Attribute the pictures with links back to the people who provided them.

When writing a post, there are a couple of things that you want to focus on to make sure that they are optimized for search engines. While this is not a 100% comprehensive guide it will certainly make your content more appealing and "relevant" to search engines. Decide on a keyword for your article. In the auto show example we are going to use "Minneapolis Auto Show" as the keyword. Remember a keyword does not refer to one word only. It can be a string of words. Now that we have defined our keywords we are going to want to use this keyword string throughout the article.

A good size blog post is a minimum of 300 words and really should be in the 500 word range. The longer the better and studies actually show that posts of 2000 to 3000 words are the most effective. I'm not trying to kill you here but people and search engines like long posts. For our example and what we generally write are 500 word posts. As a rule of thumb you want your keyword string to appear in more than 1% of the content of the article. In a 500 word post that means that the keyword should be in the article 5 times. You may need to get creative but you want to make sure you have it in there that many times.

You want to make sure that the title of you blog post contains your keyword. Not only should the title have the keyword phrase but preferably it is located in the beginning of the title. For example. "Minneapolis Auto Show Hot Cars" is better than "Cars Announced at the Minneapolis Auto Show." You also want to make sure that your title is no longer than 70 Characters. Google prefers titles under this length and will only display this many characters when showing search results.

Within the body of your blog post you will want to have headers to sections to break up the text. The headers should have the keyword if possible and be displayed as bold font. This helps make the blog post more appealing to read in addition to helping you from an SEO perspective.

Always add a photo to your blog post and make sure to incorporate the image SEO techniques we discussed earlier in the book. In summary, name the image as your keyword, add an ALT tag with the keyword, and don't be afraid to link out to the source of your image. Make sure the images you are using, are free and can be used. I like to search Flickr for images that are commercially allowed to be used. Additionally you can look for some beautiful high res images at Unsplash.

Google appreciates you linking to other sites. A well thought out site that provides valuable information for their readers naturally will have links to other sources. You should have at least one link to another site within every post. In this example maybe you will link to the Minneapolis Auto Show site directly.

"Well this sounds like an awfully large amount of work," you say. It's not, but I understand writing can seem overwhelming and it's not everyone's thing. There are options. We have also used copywriters to generate content for us in the past. This can range in quality and price and you really need to do some searching to find the right partner. Prices can range from $5 to $300 per blog post and generally speaking $15 is a fair price. You can look for writers on Fivver or Elance or even just Googling {Your Industry Copywriter}. You want to make sure they are familiar with your industry but plan on having to tweak the article after receiving it back. It will never be 100% and is going to need your involvement.

If you are concerned about receiving original content then make sure to discuss it up front with the hired copywriter. Once they return the content you can head over to a site called Copyscape. Copyscape is a huge search engine that helps ensure your content doesn't appear anywhere else online. The free version requires you to enter a web page so you may have to publish the article first and then paste the url into the box to check for plagiarism. The paid version which is incredibly cheap (couple of cents per search) allows you to actually paste the content into a box to search for uniqueness.

In summary the value of blogging is completely underestimated. Fresh content and keyword research is the easiest way to increase free traffic to your site. The other benefit to blogging is that it is around forever. Write an article or post once and it ages like fine wine ultimately attracting more and more traffic. This is a time intense exercise but one that can pay off. Remember that nothing comes quickly and not every post will be a home run but each additional visitor is another potential customer.

Backlinks

We talked previously about On-Site SEO and making sure you content is rich with keywords and relevant to your readers. This is the foundation for building good content. But how do we get the visitors and the traffic? How do we get ourselves to rank high in the search results? In order for this content to be found and be considered valuable, we need some peer recognition and endorsement.

Googles entire search algorithm was founded on the principle of backlinks. A Backlink is a link from one website to another. When someone adds a link to their site that links back to your site it is considered a backlink. Googles theory was that if someone linked to your site then they have, in a way, endorsed your site. This soft endorsement was cataloged and stored. Sites with more backlinks would show higher in the search results. The theory is that if 1 million sites linked to another website then clearly the recipient site was a more important than a site that was only linked to from 5 other sites. Therefore, they would show up higher in the search results.

In its simplicity this was the foundation for Googles search results and what largely still powers their search results today.

In addition to basic backlinks, Google went a step further and looked at the text that is used to link to your site. This was used to determine what keywords your site would show for. For example if we link to a website the actual text that has the underline and is linked is what they are looking at. ex) blue flamingoes. If a 1000 sites link to your site with the link blue flamingoes then Google correctly assumed that your site was relevant for that search query. If you had more links than a competing site with that specific set of words, you would show above them. This is the foundation of Google search and how they are able to provide more relevant links than other search engines.

As with everything though, people started to "game" the system and started creating thousands of unnatural backlinks with the terms that they wanted to rank for. The algorithm has evolved substantially over the years and now is extremely powerful. While the core principle for Google search hasn't changed, it is been refined to be incredibly smart. Google is able to review the content on the page where the link is located to make sure it's relevant to your subject and unique. They also compare sites credibility and links from more important sites carry more "link juice."

Link Juice is not an official term but it is one that is widely understood in SEO (search engine optimization) jargon. This term refers to the amount of juice you get from Google for having backlinks from various sites. A credible site carries far more link juice than a less popular site. A link from a nonprofit organization or a large news network or a government agency has an incredible amount of link juice. On the flip side a link from a user profile on a small social network or a link in a comment on a random blog post has far less juice. You are always looking to get high quality sites to link back to your site.

I know this is a lot of information. You don't have to absorb it all at once. You can spend weeks educating yourself further about backlinks and SEO. There are tons of blogs and incredible tools that will help you monitor your own links. You can go as deep as you want with this field but a basic knowledge is often satisfactory to make a big difference.

> **> WARNING <**
>
> SEO is not cheap and there is no quick fix. An effective campaign takes time and commitment. Companies will want to charge you fees monthly that are quite hefty to do lots of things you may be able to do yourself. They will provide you with fancy reports which they are generating with other sites that you have access to yourself like Moz or Ahrefs or Majestic SEO or SEMAlt

In summary, you should make an effort to get as many backlinks as you can to your site. If you are selling products for other companies make sure you get a link from those company sites. If there are local directories or organizations that you belong to, get a link from their site. These links carry lots of juice. If you want to show up prominently in search you must have lots of juicy backlinks pointing to your site. Not only do you want those links to link to your homepage but also deep into your site to specific content and product pages. Spread the love but look for backlinks wherever you can find them.

Offline Waste

Maybe you still believe in old school print advertising and you have an urge to advertise in a local paper or a local magazine. Please do me a favor and save your money. The beauty of online advertising is that it is transparent and analytical. With perfect clarity you can measure the number of people that come to your site from other sites. If you want to place a banner advertisement on another site, you can study your traffic figures and determine exactly how many people visited your site by clicking on that link. Dividing the cost per person gives you an exact number and you can determine whether or not it makes sense for you.

Offline advertising is the complete opposite. An ad in a magazine or billboard isn't measurable. This is part of the reason they are still in existence. It's clear there is a value for these placements but nobody can prove what that value is. Your optimism wants you to believe it was a good investment but the reality is, it is probably not. If you are trying to build a brand and the publication is highly targeted to your audience then it may make a good supplement to other online advertising efforts you are making. This is the one exception.

I ask you to think how often you are reading a newspaper or magazine and you are peaked by interest in an ad. You may even go ahead and fold over the page. This means I am going to come back to this. Now of those folded very hot pages you have marked, how often do you actually go online to type in the website? You don't. The numbers are abysmal and it's understandable why. As an advertiser you need to make a compelling enough pitch to have someone remember your company later at another seating when they are on the computer and then have them remember your url to go to your website. Online is instantaneous. People are interested, they click, and you have them. It's measurable and accountable and in my opinion the only thing you should be focusing on.

Get Social

Oh my. How the social world has changed and continues to change. By the time you are reading this there is no doubt a new social network that has launched that someone will be telling you that you need to pay attention to. Well here is the bad news. You need to pay attention to these social networks. I'm going to give a short breakdown of each of the top social networks and explain how they work or at least how you should be using them.

Facebook - The first and the granddaddy of all social networks, Facebook still commands attention. We talked briefly about building your audience and friending everyone you can for the launch of your new site. In addition to your personal page you will need to build a Facebook business page. This is easier than it sounds and Facebook has made it straightforward. Spend the time to dress it up and change the default images. Upload your logo and personalize the page. Facebook is one of the easiest ways to initially drive traffic to your site and to spark interest in your new site.

It takes time but one of the first things you are going to want to do once you launch your site is to invite all of your friends to like your business page. This is your chance to get them captive and be able to communicate your message to them. You will still be able to post company information to your individual page but far less frequently then you will be doing on your business page. It is a courtesy and most people understand that business is business and pleasure is pleasure. You will need to toe the line and do what you are comfortable with.

Your posts to Facebook should be engaging and include a picture. People are lazy and prefer to look rather than read. When they are scrolling through their timeline you want your image to stand out. Ideally you are posting once a day or every other day. Don't panic. We will explain shortly how you can tie these social networks together which will save you substantial time. This allows you to post to one network and have it published on others.

Facebook is huge and can be a major generator of traffic to your site. In the last couple of years they have released Facebook ads which allows you to show your ads to a highly targeted demographic of users. The beauty of Facebook is that they know just about everything about their users. Because they have this information, you are able to target specific viewers. For example if you sold baby clothes only in Florida you could target women who make above a certain income level, that have a child, shop online and are based in Florida. You can see that this is incredibly powerful.

Facebook advertising similar to Google AdWords is CPC (cost per click) and you can determine what you are willing to pay for clicks and monitor conversions to determine what a visitor is worth to you. It is transparent and endlessly configurable which makes it a powerful option for advertising.

> WARNING <

Because of Facebooks size and reach its incredibly important that you pay attention when you setup your ad campaign. Its much easier to tightly define your group and loosen up the restrictions once you have had a chance to gauge response. If you leave it loose and don't set a limit on spending you can blow through a lot of money very quickly to unqualified visitors.

Twitter - Twitter was the other major social network that still has an incredible following with millions and millions of engaged users. Twitter famously only allows you to enter 140 characters. People follow you and others, and as you tweet or post something to twitter, it appears in their timeline. It is a real-time information sharing tool. The nature of twitter though is that people come in and out of their timeline based on when they have time. They are often following lots of people and may or may not see your tweet.

Some people will use tools like HootSuite or Buffer. This allows you to pre-schedule your tweets in advance. You can enter them and set the time of day and day that you would like them shared. You can configure how many times to share it and gives you the ability to automate a lot of your tweeting work. Again this can be connected from your Facebook page or vice versa so that you can share to one platform and have it post or update to the others.

Twitter also offers advertising in the form of promoted tweets. Similar to the other social networks you can set up a campaign to target the demographic of the user you would like. You also can set a price you are willing to pay per engagement. An engagement is defined as a retweet (sharing your tweet), a favorite or a click through the link in your tweet. This saves you a lot of money and again plays into accountability and only paying for actual performance.

Twitter as opposed to other social networks is predominantly text messages that are being shared. While you can embed a picture or video clip, the primary share is done in simple 140 character sentences. This is extremely effective for products or services that are less visual in nature but may have proven results or facts to share. Twitter is a great outlet for that type of offering.

Instagram - Also owned by Facebook, Instagram is one of the fastest growing social networks. Similar to twitter you follow people and are followed by others. Images you post show up in followers timelines. Instagram is photo driven. Every post to Instagram must include a photo or video and can include a sentence, hashtags, and mentions of other people.

Instagram is an extremely effective tool for brands with products that are visual in nature. People like to see products being used or worn. Instagram also allows others to see third party endorsements. When photos are liked or commented on, people feel comfortable because others are endorsing the product or service. It puts a name and a voice to a brand.

With time and effort you can successfully build a large audience which can prove to be a powerful sales channel to your site. One thing to note is that Instagram does not allow you to insert links in your post. The only place to put a link is in your profile. Make sure you have a link there. Another point of interest is that Instagram cannot be posted to from other social networks. You must start your post in Instagram and then share to other social networks from Instagram.

LinkedIn - LinkedIn is the more professional social network. There is less personal sharing and primarily business discussions and connections through LinkedIn. You create your resume and are able to connect or Link with other people you know. You are then able to communicate and contact people that may be 1 or 2 connections removed from you.

LinkedIn works incredibly well for B2B (business to business) sales like consulting or business product offerings. They offer paid plans where you can communicate with people that you may not have had contact information for. Although not a direct driver of traffic to your site LinkedIn can help you build your business network and open doors for more involved sales you are looking to make.

Google + - In an effort to compete with Facebook and many of the other social networks, Google launched Google + in 2011. Because of Googles sheer size they were able to indirectly sign people up for Google + through one of the many other products they offer. They claim to have over a half a billion active users and because of their network of other solutions they may.

While Google + is something that you have to pay attention to, it is somewhat of a mystery. It is the behemoth of social networks that nobody is really using. The idea was novel in the sense that you were able to create circles. Circles are defined as groups of people in your life that share something in common. For example work people or family or your bowling team. You are able to share across these circles keeping private items to just the circles you want to share with.

My completely unscientific research shows that Google + is good for one thing. That one thing is showing Google that you are using it. Posting to Google +, creating a business page and linking it to your website and following other people has shown to increase your search engine rankings. These positive impacts to your search results are reason enough to use Google +.

While some of you may use Google + more effectively or be able to build a group of people that are meaningfully sharing content and connecting with others, I'm convinced it needs a major overhaul or will fall into obsolescence. With that said, Google is Google and therefore you don't want to upset the gorilla. Create a profile, create a business page and make a point to share. If nothing else share links to pages on your site for some nice backlinks.

Pinterest - Used primarily by woman, Pinterest is an incredible way to drive traffic to your products. Pinterest allows you to create an account and create boards. Boards are collections of images that you can organize from around the web. Let's say for example someone is going on vacation and wants to create a board called "Vacation Spots." They would then browse the internet and when they come across an image of a vacation spot they like they will "pin it." Using a button in their browser or on the site, the image would be saved on their board.

The beauty of these boards are that almost all of them are public and other users can find your boards and posts on those boards. Each post has a description and a link back to the original source of the image. This is a backlink (has little juice) but more importantly it drives highly targeted traffic to your site and to the specific product pages.

For example if you sell sneakers, you may create a board called basketball sneakers and then pin all of your individual styles to this board. People who browse or search Pinterest will find your sneakers. They may actually click through and purchase them on your site or maybe just repin your post to their board. This is then shared with their followers and on it goes.

Take the time to pin your products to Pinterest. Each and every one from its own individual page should be pinned to a board. You will be surprised at the longevity or this one time action. People will favorite and repin and this will continue to drive traffic to your site.

Pinterest also offers Promoted Pins. Similar to Facebook ads and Google AdWords you can put a bid or price you are willing to pay for your pin to show above others in peoples searches. You are only charged when people click on your ads but not when ads are repinned or viewed. This is another affordable avenue to advertise products in your store. On some products we are seeing costs as low as 5 cents per click. For 5 cents we're happy to have a visitor to the website.

Tumblr - More of a blog type platform, Tumblr is a little different than the other social networks we have outlined above. Tumblr lets you create a page and then add posts to your site. You also can follow other users and see their posts but it is made for a more long form type of content sharing. Generally Tumblr posts are longer and more of a blog forum.

If you are already blogging on your site this may be redundant to setup and have but if you connect it to one of the other social platforms that you will be sharing to, it is an easy way to build another page of content that will be discoverable in the search engines and furthermore have backlinks to your site.

Hashtags - You have heard of them before but maybe you aren't exactly sure what a hashtag is. A hashtag is actually a tag that you can add to a post that you put on social networks. Hashtags basically group items so that users can search or view similar items on social networks. A hashtag is created by entering a pound sign # and then any other word or group of words after it.

For example let's say we were selling dog clothes online and we wanted to post a picture of a new dog sweater that we had in our store. We could write something like "I love this new sweater we just got in." We would then add some hashtags to the end of the sentence like #dogsweater #dogclothes. There are no spaces in hashtags.

By adding the hashtag to the end of your sentence you have tagged your post with these terms. This helps your information become searchable. Now that the data has been tagged when someone searches for dog sweater within the social network you posted, your post will show. Often times you can just click on the hashtag and you will see all results within that social network with similar hashtags.

In a sea of a million posts a second, if you are not adding hashtags, your information becomes very difficult to be found. Of course they will show in the feeds of the people that are following you but you are trying to find new people that may be searching random hashtags or viewing similar posts to a hashtag they may have used.

In the dog sweater scenario maybe someone has just posted a picture of their dog wearing a dog sweater on their way to the dog park. They coincidentally tag their post #dogsweater and share it. After they post, they click on the hashtag #dogsweater to see what other posts come up and sure enough your new post for your new dog sweater shows up. They click through, fall in love and buy your sweater on your site. This is how you can help increase engagement, traffic and followers on your social networks.

Get creative with your hashtags so that you can hopefully reach as many people as possible. Use the city name you are posting from or a feeling you are having. Hashtags started on Twitter but have become so popular, they have been universally implemented across, Instagram, Tumblr, Google +, Facebook, Pinterest and many others.

Connecting Them All
It is overwhelming. I just laid out half a dozen social networks and if you spent time doing all of them I'm not sure you could get anything else done. The ones I listed is just the tip of the iceberg and there are many others that people are using. The good news is you don't have to know them all. For the ones that you do decide to use, there is a way to tie these all together. This lets you post to one network and most of the others are updated. Depending on your offering you will want to concentrate on a particular platform and really make that your primary platform.

For the sake of this example we will consider a standard e commerce product offering. For this we will focus on Instagram. Instagram allows you to post your product image and message and then share the same message to a number of other platforms. From Instagram you can share to

Facebook, Tumblr, Twitter, Flickr and Foursquare. This means that when you post your image and message on Instagram the same image and comments will be sent to these other social networks if you so choose. This results in multiple updates across multiple social networks to reach more people all with one post.

The hashtags will work within the different platforms and although Instagram doesn't allow a link to be clickable others networks do. When writing your post include your url and share to the other platforms. It will appear as clickable and counted as a backlink when posted on Facebook and Tumblr and Twitter.

Something to note when sharing from Instagram to twitter is that the image will show as a link and not the actual image. The engagement is much lower and you really want the whole image natively embed in twitter. Here is how you can do it. Instead of sharing directly to twitter from Instagram try using IFTTT . IFTTT allows you to setup automated procedures. When you sign up for a free account, you will search for the Instagram to twitter recipe. You will login to both services and enable the recipe. This enables every post from Instagram to be properly posted to twitter with the full image. Its automatic and once you set it, you can forget it.

Google + unfortunately is the one social network that doesn't play nicely when sharing information. You will still need to post manually to Google +. They purposely haven't given users a way to connect other services to post to Google +. Google in their quest for more original content wants to prevent duplicate content and force you to provide a unique post on Google +. Unfortunately this means in order to stay up to date there, you will have to post yourself on Google +.

With these combinations though and many others on IFTTT or Hoot Suite or others, you are able to dramatically consolidate the amount of work needed to stay current each day often with one or two posts.

Google Alerts

Google has a great little tool that most people haven't heard of. It is called Google Alerts. Google Alerts allows you to setup a notification. Either daily or weekly or in real time you can be notified at no cost for mentions of your brand or name online. Google Alerts lets you enter whatever terms you want. It will then scour the internet and any mentions of your brand or personal name will be emailed to you with a link to the post. This is a great tool that is completely free. Stay on top what people are saying about you or your brand.

Just Google It

One of the most important things you are going to need to learn if you haven't already is the power of the internet. Clearly you understand how amazing it is, but don't forget that anything you are looking for is online. While starting your ecommerce business may seem a daunting task, there are answers at your fingertips. Anything you do or have questions about, someone has done or asked about it themselves. You need to learn to Google your problems away. Don't know how to crop and image? Google It. Don't know how to right align something? Google It. Just Google It.

There are countless forums and how-to guides offered for free with incredible detail of how to resolve whatever problem you are having. Don't get discouraged. If you can't find your answer, rephrase your search and try again. Google is an incredible tool that puts you on an equal playing field as anyone else. If you can't find what you are looking for, give it rest. Come back and hour later and search again. It is there and you can fix just about any problem with the help of Google.

[4]
Converting and Maximizing Your Revenue

Email Lists

We have talked about the importance of email list and building your list as soon as you can. What we haven't talked about are how to get these emails. One of the best ways to collect emails is asking people who actually visit your site to join your list. As with anything in this world, people naturally want to know what's in it for them by joining your list. Rightfully so, they need to be sold on why they should be joining your list and what exactly you are going to provide them with. Maybe your pitch of special sales and notifications is enough but we have seen time and time again that something of value is the best way to have people opt in to your email list. This may be a guide or ebook or a discount code or something related to your topic to entice them to join.

Once you have decided what exactly you are going to give them in return, you need to decide how to get them to opt in. One of the most effective ways to get them to sign up is to ask them. How exactly do you ask them though if you are not speaking with them? The answer is the icky popup. I know you may not like popups. The problem is that they are effective. They are effective and that is why you are seeing them everywhere. You don't need to require people to opt in but if you don't ask, you won't get.

There are a number of different ways to implement this functionality. Some people subtly have opt in portions or input boxes on their homepage or in the footer of their site. Unfortunately these are far less effective than the annoying ones. There are a number of companies that focus on these annoying popups. They allow you to handle popups or slide outs from the side of the screen or top of the screen. You can prompt people with the pop-up immediately upon landing on your site or you can delay it to give the user some time. There are endless options here. You can take a look at Lead Pages or Drip or Optin Monster or you can actually use the free "evil popup" form from Mailchimp that will allow you to do it yourself.

The key is to start somewhere. You need to start building your list and without asking for email addresses you can't begin to build it.

The Drips

Well now you have a list of email addresses and it is time to do something with them. Studies have shown that most people will not purchase something on their first interaction with your company. It can take as many as 3 or 4 contact points before someone feels comfortable enough to actually purchase something. Now that you have their email address its time to do that.

You should be emailing an offer or newsletter on a regular basis. These constant touch points start to build trust and move people towards purchasing from you. However, I understand that this takes time and commitment and maybe you aren't sending out emails as frequently as you would like to. Maybe you are only sending a newsletter or email blast every other month. That is not going to cut it and you probably have lost the initial interest you had from your new registration by then.

The answer is something referred to as a drip campaign. The idea of a drip campaign is that you pre-write a multi-part email series. You then schedule these emails to be sent at planned time intervals that you determine. For example, you send an initial welcome email upon their signup to your list. You then may send a second email 3 or 4 days later followed by a couple others after that. You can work on these emails and refine them.

The content of these emails really depend on your particular offering. Let's say for this example you have a site selling auto accessories. Maybe you entice people to sign up for your email list in exchange for a 5 part crash course in maintaining your car. You can structure 5 emails and save the upsell for the last email. This way you are building trust with your customer and giving them information. By the last email you are letting them know special accessories that your store offers to help them maintain their car.

These drips can be scheduled through your email service provider like Constant Contact or AWeber or MailChimp or you can use a company like Get Drip which will let you setup your scheduled emails and control more details of the Drip campaign. All of these options will show advanced reporting of opens and clicks for each campaign.

Offers and Urgency

Unfortunately today's consumer has become a creature of habit. Bad habits at that. I was reading Fortune magazine the other day and there was an article about how sales are now the expected norm. People find themselves waiting only for sales because they have been trained to buy during sales. This means that if you don't have a special offer or incentive to purchase, it is becoming harder and harder to get someone motivated to actually pull out their credit card.

Given that people are now creatures of habit, it is important to play into that psychology. After countless sales and offers and promotions, I can tell you that there are a couple of crucial elements to a successful sale or offering. Scarcity and Exclusiveness are up at the top. You need to make your offer limited whether that's limited by time or availability and you need to make it feel exclusive. Let's take a look at some good and bad tag lines or offers that can help move the needle.

GOOD: The first 10 people to purchase with the promocode XXXX will get $20 offer any purchase over $100.

BAD: Use the promocode XXXX and save $20.

GOOD: Use discount code VIP before Sunday to save $20 off your purchase. Please don't distribute this code as its for select recipients.

BAD: Use discount code EVERBODYSAVES any time in January to save $20 off your purchase.

People also need to be reminded over and over again. If you are having a weekend sale then tell them before the weekend and don't be afraid to let them know when it is ending. Remind them it is their last chance. You don't have to use email for all these notifications but hopefully through your social media or other means you are able to touch them a couple of times during your sale. You want to make sure that anyone on the fence makes a purchase. People want to feel special and don't want to be left out. Play to that weakness.

Partnering and Affiliates

To effectively build your business you need to get the word out to as many people as possible. This may mean that you need to start locally and offline to get the word out. It is going to take time to spread the word about your business online so you need to make sure everyone in your local area knows as well. Although we don't believe advertising offline is money well spent, there are offline opportunities to make money. You need to make sales any way you can when starting out. Money allows you to increase your inventory and add new products or services. This creates hype and allows you to expand your reach. Once you reach a point where you are generating enough online sales, you can stop this. You started and online business to sell online. Selling any way you can will help you reach that goal more quickly.

In order to sell offline without a retail location you are going to have to look for partnerships. You are going to need to incentivize people to work with them. Nothing does that like money. There are endless ways to co-op or dream of ways to partner with local businesses or people to help get your brand and site in as many people's hands as possible. The first thing to think about is how you can make partnerships that are mutually beneficial for both of you. The best partnerships are ones that make sense for everyone.

Let's consider some examples and you can then see how they may translate to your business. Let's assume you have a website for pet supplies. You sell all types of pet clothes and toys. Your first bet is to think where your target audience can be found. Your audience is anyone who owns a pet. Well we know people will be at a pet store but that is probably not such a good idea because the pet store is probably selling many of the same items you are selling. Next thing that comes to mind are vets offices. It is a safe bet that people at the vets' office have a pet and are potential customers.

The next step is to think how you can partner with the vets office to make something beneficial for both the vets office and your site. I can only guess because I'm not a vet but, I imagine Vets have a couple of interests that may motivate them.

1.   Obtaining additional clients and spreading the word about their services.
2.   Increasing their bottom line through additional revenue streams.
3.   Raising money for local charities or animal shelters.

Now that we have isolated these assumptions, we can construct a partnership that will benefit them in one of these three ways, if not more. First we could offer them to have a special event at their office on their busiest day. You would bring your products in and set up a table in their reception area to sell your products. You can offer them a share of the revenue generated. Additionally you will email your whole local list of contacts to have them come to learn more about the vets' office. They can give their literature away alongside your material. Customers are entertained while they wait to see the vet and some excitement is brought to the office. If they don't want to take a revenue share they may elect to donate it to a local animal shelter. You can possibly tie in an animal shelter and tell the shelter that you will be giving 10% of the proceeds to their shelter. In exchange for the donation you would only ask that they send out an email to their email list advising people of the event. The vet gets the free advertising by hosting the event and being included in the email.

This is a perfect example of a win, win, win for three separate parties. The Vet gets excitement, new visitors, advertising in your email and the non-profits email, and additional revenue. The non-profit gets additional awareness from clients of the vet as well as proceeds from your sales. Last and not least you will make sales and get your name out to the vets' clients and the non-profit members. I understand this is not an easy thing to orchestrate but it is an example of how you can partner with different companies and be creative in building partnerships that are beneficial for all of those involved.

A more streamlined conventional partnership online often involves an affiliate program. Somebody adds a link to their website or a banner advertisement on their site or email blast that points their guests to your business. A unique tracking url (ex: http://www.petclothes.com/?referral=dave) is used so that you can track the traffic from Dave. If any sales are made you will share the revenue with Dave. You can customize these agreements any way that you want but essentially they are revenue share models. If you are looking for affiliate advertisers or are considering advertising your products through an affiliate model we would recommend you take a look at Share a Sale. There are other companies that are bigger and more well known like Commission Junction and Link Share but their costs are substantially higher.

Amazon is probably the most well-known company to use a complex affiliate program. They have a huge market of little advertisers actively marketing their products in exchange for a cut of the revenue. Here is our Amazon affiliate link. We greatly appreciate if you click through and buy something.

If you are looking for a basic beginner's setup of an affiliate program you can implement an affiliate program by using one of the many shopping cart plugins that already exist. There are hundreds of WordPress plugins that will handle this for you and Shopify and the other shopping cart solutions also offer a myriad of affiliate program plugins. I am not comfortable unfortunately referring you to a specific one as I don't have firsthand experience using them. I have always used a custom built solution or a variation on the affiliate program.

The variation that we have successfully used is an exclusive coupon code. You use the coupon code as an affiliate referral tracker. Most if not all of the shopping cart solutions come with the ability to offer coupon codes. The coupon codes are designed to give the consumer a discount on their purchase at the store. We use this coupon functionality to help track referrals.

The best way to get someone to actually use a tracking code is by giving them a benefit to use it. For example if you partner with a blogger who is going to write a piece about your new online business. You can reach out to the blogger and say in exchange for an article on their site, you are willing to give them a unique coupon code. For their readers who use the coupon code, they will get x% off when they use the coupon and as a side incentive you are going to pay the blogger y% of any sales made with that coupon code. It is a simple way to track referrals and also offer an additional benefit for the blogger to be able to offer their readers.

There are endless ways to come up with creative partnerships whether they are at brick and mortar locations or they are online based through tracking coupon codes. You need to be creative and create a list of all the potential places and organizations that have groups of people that would are potential customers. Once you have the list, then write down the things that most likely would benefit these people. Now that you have a list of target companies, organizations, or people and their specific trigger points, then you can tailor an offering that makes sense for both of you. Get creative, think outside of the box and go for it. What's the worst they can say? No Thank You?

Trade shows

We talked about partnering with local businesses as a way to get more exposure for your site and jump start traffic and brand awareness but there are many other avenues. You may be hesitant to make an effort to sell offline. I understand. You didn't start a retail store and why should you do it. It is a lot of work and not the business you wanted to start. I hear you, but. The internet is a big place and you have to start somewhere. The best place to start spreading the word is locally and that means through email lists, partnerships, flyers, and Bazaars/Trade Shows.

Depending on your product or service, you will be able to find local trade shows or bazaars where you can rent a booth to exhibit and sell your product or service. These can be very successful or a terrible waste of money. You need to do some due diligence up front to make sure you are not wasting your time or money. These trade shows and bazaars have different setups and arrangements. Some require you to rent the space as well as tables, equipment, power and every imaginable supply from them. Others want a percentage of your sales at the event. They each are structured a little differently and you need to make sure they are going to work for you.

Find out who is going to be there and how many are expected to attend. Find out if they did it last year and ask around to see if you know anyone who participated last year. Hearing first hand from them whether or not it was worthwhile is priceless. You can save time and money asking up front. Regardless when you attend these events, it's important to remember your goal is twofold. You are looking to generate sales and make money to expand your inventory and advertising funds. More importantly you are trying to drive traffic to your online site.

The purpose of attending these events is to get your name out there.

You should have printed flyers to hand to people that have your website on them and other social network accounts. Stamp your box and packaging. If you are putting things in a bag, make sure you website is listed on there. Collect emails and add people to your list. Your most important goal is to make sure they understand you are an online store and to get them to go online. You have to start spreading the word and putting your brand and website address in their hands. This helps drive that traffic you are looking for.

Customer Service

One of the most important parts of growing your online business is ensuring all of your customers love you and the experience of purchasing from you. Your initial year of sales is extremely important in setting the tone as to the experience you want your customers to have. If they have a problem, you need to resolve it. This may mean that you resolve it at a loss to the company. The online world is enormous but an unhappy customer can create a lot of trouble for you. Is it worth not accepting a return to have someone post terrible feedback on message boards? You need to protect your reputation closely.

Be proud of what you are sending and the packaging you are sending it in. All of these little details set the tone for what people can expect. Make a professional presentation and handle people professionally. Go the extra step, send an email thanking someone with a coupon code your past customers. If someone had a bad experience even if by no fault of yours, make it right for them. Give them a discount code on their next purchase or waive the shipping costs. These little gestures leave a nice taste in someone's mouth and helps spread the word about your business. American Express in a recent study found that on average, happy customers tell an average of 9 people about their experience. Repeat business and word of mouth is the fastest way to help grow your business.

You made it

You did it. You have taken the first step in launching your ecommerce business successfully. There is a lot of information in this book and it is not designed to be read once and put aside. You can't possibly remember all of the details we have outlined for you in this book. This book is designed to be used as a reference. You can refer back to any of the sections to further familiarize yourself with the details of a particular chapter. The good news is that you have read through at least once. You are familiar with the overall goal and how to get there.

Now it is up to you. You may have read a number of books and been to a number of meet-ups or discussions with other people about starting your business. It is time to act. Stop procrastinating and setting arbitrary dates. There will never be an optimal time or date and there will always be another milestone that you can wait for. If you have read through the book and are prepared for the work involved then just do it already. If you get stuck you can always just Google it.

Postscript Thank You

You made it. Good for you. Now its time to put this in action. Don't worry we won't leave you alone. We are blogging weekly with ideas and further tests that we are doing and you can follow along at
http://www.longlivetheinternet.com

Lastly if you haven't downloaded our free resource guide gift, you can do this now at
http://www.longlivetheinternet.com/book-gift

Made in the USA
Lexington, KY
20 July 2016